Spanish

THE AUSTRALIAN
Women's Weekly

Spanish

acp books

Contents

Tapas – those small dishes of highly seasoned appetisers – have become the most famous and best-loved of all Spanish food. There are tapas bars springing up in cities all around the world. And it's not surprising that these morsels, usually eaten with a glass of wine or sherry before dinner, are now universally enjoyed. They can be served not only as appetisers, but you can make a whole meal of tapas, you can cater for a wedding with tapas – they're extremely versatile and incredibly appealing.

But of course Spanish food is not just made up of tapas. Seafood plays a big part in the Spanish repertoire – prawns, sardines, octopus and squid most commonly. Rice, chickpeas and beans are eaten extensively – paella is the most well-known of Spanish rice dishes. Pork is popular, especially when made into chorizo sausage – a delicious spicy sausage that features in many Spanish dishes. There are some great chicken and quail dishes too and vegetables are found in soups, paella, salads and as a wonderful little course all on their own.

Of Spanish desserts, flan is probably the most famous (a kind of crème caramel) but there are also churros, deep-fried pastries that are irresistible and often eaten for breakfast dipped into hot chocolate, and there's also a delicious creamy rice pudding.

Spanish food is made for communal eating – it's light, fresh and very healthy, often cooked in the olive oil from the region – it's the perfect excuse to get together with family and friends and indulge in a long Spanish lunch.

Spanish essentials

CHORIZO
Are small, coarse-textured pork and beef sausages. They are deeply smoked, very spicy and dry-cured so that they do not need cooking. Serve chorizo cold with bread, pickled vegetables and a glass of sherry as a tapas dish, or grilled or fried and served hot. Chorizo can also be purchased as a fresh sausage.

OLIVE OIL
Available in several grades, virgin oils are the best. Extra virgin and virgin oils are best used for salad oils and gentle frying of delicate foods. "Pure olive oil" (or simply "olive oil"), is usually a mixture of virgin and refined oil, and is best for general frying. Spain produces one third of the world's olive oil.

PAPRIKA
Paprika is made from the dried ground fruits of several members of the capsicum/chilli family. There are many grades and types available depending on the fruit from which it is made, including sweet, hot, mild and smoked. Paprika produced in Spain is particularly fine and is an important ingredient in romesco sauce.

PAELLA RICE (CALASPARRA)
This Spanish short-grain rice absorbs three times its own volume of liquid, while keeping its firm shape; perfectly suited to making paella. The two specialist varieties are calasparra and bomba (grown in Calasparra), and are cultivated by hand; quality of production is protected by Denominación de Origen standards.

OLIVES

Olives are eaten green (unripe) and black (ripe). Both are inedibly bitter when picked and must be leached of their bitter juices by salt-curing or brining. Green olives are firm and tangy; available pitted, stone-in or stuffed. Black olives are more mellow in flavour than green ones and are softer in texture; available stone-in, pitted and sliced.

SARDINES & ANCHOVIES

Small oily fish. Sardines are commonly purchased canned (tightly packed in oil or brine); fresh sardines are also available and grilled, pickled or smoked. Anchovy fillets are preserved and packed in oil or salt in small cans or jars, and are strong in flavour. Fresh anchovies are much milder in flavour.

JAMON

A specialist Spanish cured ham, there are two distinctive types: jamón serrano, which is dry-cured for at least a year giving it a deep flavour and firm texture; and jamón ibérico, produced from the black Iberian pig, which is intense and complex in flavour.

SAFFRON

The stigma (three per flower) of the saffron crocus. It imparts a yellow-orange colour to food once infused – use with restraint as too much can overwhelm other flavours. Quality can vary greatly and the best is the most expensive spice in the world. Nearly three-quarters of the world's saffron production comes from Spain.

MANCHEGO CHEESE
A famous semi-firm Spanish sheep's cheese which is mild when young, but after ageing for 3 months or longer, becomes a rich golden colour and develops a full, tangy flavour with the characteristic aftertaste of sheep's milk.

CAPSICUM (BELL PEPPER)
Capsicum belong to the same family as hot chillies, but do not contain heat. This heatless fruit is known as pimiento in Spain. Capsicums are green when unripe, and ripen to red, yellow, purple-black or brown. Canned red ones are available, often imported under its Spanish name pimiento.

SHERRY & SHERRY VINEGAR
A fortified wine made from white grapes grown near Jerez, Spain. Stored in American oak casks, it is aged in the solera system (where new wine is periodically added and moved progressively through a series of barrels). Sherry is aged this way for a minimum of 3 years; sherry vinegar from Jerez is aged this way for an average of 6 years.

ALMONDS
Flat, pointy-tipped nut with a pitted brown shell; its creamy white kernel is covered by a brown skin. Mild in flavour when raw, roasting brings out a warm, embracing flavour. They are available in the shell, as whole kernels (raw or roasted), blanched (kernels, skins removed), flaked (paper-thin slices), slivered (pieces cut lengthways), and ground.

ORANGES

The most popular citrus fruit, oranges are available all year round. There are two main kinds of orange: sweet (navel, valencia, blood oranges) and bitter (seville). Oranges will keep well for a few days at room temperature; for longer storage, store in the refrigerator.

CHICKPEAS (GARBANZO BEANS)

An irregularly round, sandy-coloured legume used extensively in Mediterranean, Indian and Hispanic cooking. They have a firm texture even after cooking, a floury mouth-feel and robust nutty flavour. Available canned (pre-cooked) or dried (must be soaked in water for several hours before cooking).

CINNAMON

Available in pieces (sticks or quills) and ground; it is one of the world's most common spices and is used as a sweet, fragrant flavouring. True cinnamon is the dried inner bark of the shoots of the Sri Lankan native cinnamon tree; it is often blended with cassia (chinese cinnamon) to produce "cinnamon" commonly found in supermarkets.

SEAFOOD

With its extensive coastline, fresh seafood is an important element of Spanish cuisine. Fish, prawns, mussels, clams, octopus and squid (to name just a few) are prominent, and commonly used in well-known Spanish dishes such as paella.

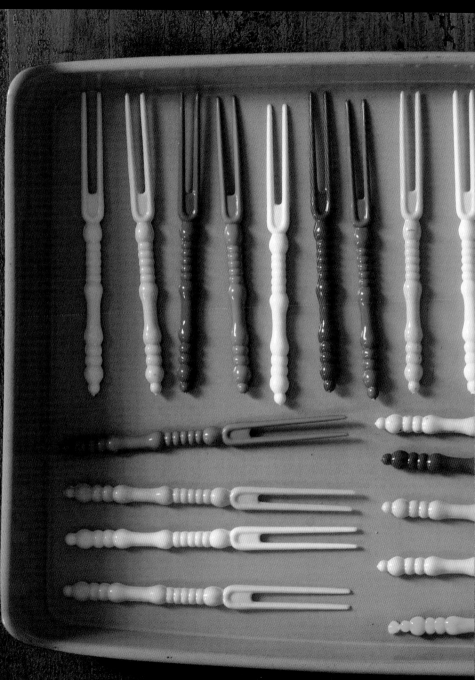

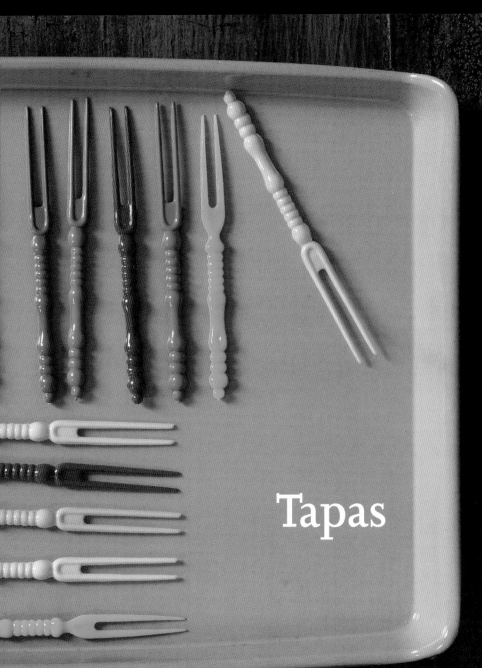

Tapas

Sangria

6 whole cloves
1 cinnamon stick
¼ cup (55g) caster (superfine) sugar
3 cups (750ml) orange juice
½ cup (125ml) port
10cm (4-inch) thin strip orange rind
3 cups (750ml) light red wine
½ cup (125ml) brandy
½ cup (125ml) gin
½ cup (125ml) vermouth
⅓ cup (80ml) grenadine
1.25 litres (5 cups) lemonade
1 large orange (300g), quartered, sliced thinly
1 large red apple (200g), quartered, cored, sliced thinly

1 Stir spices, sugar, juice, port and rind in medium saucepan over heat, without boiling, until sugar is dissolved. Simmer, uncovered, 5 minutes, strain into large heatproof bowl; cool.
2 Add wine, brandy, gin, vermouth, grenadine, lemonade and orange to juice mixture. Cover; refrigerate 3 hours or overnight.
3 Add apple just before serving.

prep + cook time 15 minutes (+ cooling & refrigeration)
makes 3.5 litres (14 cups)
nutritional count per 1 cup (250ml) 0.1g total fat (0g saturated fat); 769kJ (184 cal); 25.4g carbohydrate; 0.7g protein; 0.8g fibre
tip We used a pinot noir-style red wine in this version of the traditional recipe.

White sangria

2 large green apples (400g), unpeeled, sliced thinly
½ cup (125ml) lime juice
1.5 litres (6 cups) riesling
½ cup (125ml) white rum
⅓ cup (80ml) apple schnapps
½ cup (80g) pure icing (confectioners') sugar
3 cups (525g) seedless green grapes, halved
2 cups (300g) fresh blueberries
3 cups (750ml) sparkling mineral water
ice cubes, for serving

1 Place apple in medium bowl with juice; stand 5 minutes.
2 Place undrained apples in large jug with remaining ingredients; stir to combine. Cover; refrigerate 3 hours or overnight.
3 Add ice to jug just before serving.

prep time 10 minutes (+ refrigeration) **makes** 3 litres (12 cups)
nutritional count per 1 cup (250ml) 0.1g total fat (0g saturated fat); 869kJ (208 cal); 22.4g carbohydrate; 0.8g protein; 1.4g fibre
tip Only fresh blueberries can be used in this recipe because frozen berries will tint the sangria.

Olives with caperberries and sherry vinegar

1¼ cups (150g) green olives
1 cup (160g) rinsed drained caperberries
5 sprigs fresh lemon thyme
¼ cup (60ml) sherry vinegar
¾ cup (180ml) olive oil

1 Combine ingredients in medium bowl. Cover; refrigerate overnight or up to 1 week.

prep time 15 minutes (+ refrigeration) **serves** 8
nutritional count per serving 21.6g total fat (3.1g saturated fat); 932kJ (223 cal); 7.3g carbohydrate; 0.3g protein; 0.6g fibre

Martini olives

370g (12 ounces) canned anchovy-stuffed green manzanilla olives,
    rinsed, drained
1 tablespoon finely chopped fresh rosemary
4 fresh bay leaves
1 tablespoon extra dry vermouth
1 tablespoon gin
½ cup (125ml) olive oil

1 Combine ingredients in medium bowl. Cover; refrigerate overnight or
up to 1 week. Serve olives with crusty bread.

prep time 15 minutes (+ refrigeration) **serves** 8
nutritional count per serving 17.3g total fat (2.5g saturated fat);
711kJ (170 cal); 0.7g carbohydrate; 0.3g protein; 2.9g fibre
tip Spanish anchovy-stuffed green manzanilla olives can be found at
specialty food stores and delicatessens. If you can't find them, use any
green olives you like.

Garlic and paprika char-grilled prawns

12 uncooked medium king prawns (shrimp) (540g)
1 medium red capsicum (bell pepper) (200g), chopped coarsely
⅓ cup (80ml) olive oil
2 cloves garlic, crushed
1 teaspoon smoked paprika

1 Shell and devein prawns, leaving tails intact.
2 Combine prawns, capsicum, oil, garlic and paprika in medium bowl; season.
3 Cook capsicum on heated grill plate (or grill or barbecue) until browned both sides. Add prawns towards the end of capsicum cooking time; cook, turning, until prawns change colour.
4 Serve with lemon wedges, if you like.

prep + cook time 30 minutes **serves** 6
nutritional count per serving 12.5g total fat (1.8g saturated fat); 652kJ (156 cal); 1.2g carbohydrate; 9.7g protein; 0.5g fibre

Prawns with fresh tomato sauce

12 uncooked medium king prawns (shrimp) (540g)
2 tablespoons olive oil
4 cloves garlic, sliced thinly
4 medium vine-ripened tomatoes (420g), chopped coarsely
2 teaspoons red wine vinegar
1 tablespoon coarsely chopped fresh flat-leaf parsley

1 Shell and devein prawns, leaving tails intact.
2 Heat oil in large frying pan; cook garlic until browned lightly.
Add tomato; cook, uncovered, stirring occasionally, about 5 minutes.
Add prawns and vinegar; cook until prawns change colour. Season to
taste; stir in parsley.
3 Serve prawns with crusty bread.

prep + cook time 25 minutes **serves** 6
nutritional count per serving 6.5g total fat (0.9g saturated fat);
447kJ (107 cal); 1.5g carbohydrate; 10.1g protein; 1.2g fibre

Grilled mussels with jamón

20 small black mussels (500g)
2 cups (500ml) water
80g (2½ ounces) butter, softened
50g (1½ ounces) thinly sliced jamón, chopped finely
1 clove garlic, crushed
2 green onions (scallions), chopped finely

1 Scrub mussels; remove beards. Bring the water to the boil in large saucepan. Add the mussels, cover; boil about 3 minutes or until mussels open (discard any that do not).
2 Drain mussels; discard liquid. Break open shells; discard top shell. Loosen mussels from shells with a spoon; return mussels to shells, place in single layer on oven tray.
3 Preheat grill (broiler).
4 Combine butter, jamón, garlic and onion in small bowl. Divide butter mixture over mussels; grill about 3 minutes or until browned lightly.

prep + cook time 30 minutes **serves** 4
nutritional count per serving 17.6g total fat (11.2g saturated fat); 773kJ (185 cal); 1.8g carbohydrate; 5.5g protein; 0.2g fibre
tip Jamón is a type of Spanish cured ham, similar to prosciutto. It is available in specialty delicatessens. Use prosciutto if you can't get it.

Cod and olive fritters

650g (1 ¼ pounds) salted cod fillet, skin on
3 medium potatoes (600g), halved
1 tablespoon olive oil
1 medium brown onion (150g), chopped finely
2 cloves garlic, crushed
¼ cup finely chopped fresh flat-leaf parsley
½ cup (60g) seeded green olives, chopped finely
1 egg
vegetable oil, for deep-frying

1 Rinse fish under cold water to remove excess salt. Place fish in large bowl, cover with cold water; refrigerate, covered, overnight, changing the water three or four times. Drain fish; discard water.
2 Place fish in large saucepan, cover with cold water; bring to the boil uncovered. Reduce heat; simmer, covered, 5 minutes. Drain fish, discard water; remove skin and bones then flake fish.
3 Boil, steam or microwave potato until tender; drain. Roughly mash potato in large bowl.
4 Meanwhile, heat olive oil in large frying pan; cook onion and garlic, stirring, until onion softens.
5 Combine fish, onion mixture, parsley, olives and egg with potato.
6 Roll level tablespoons of fish mixture into balls, place on baking-paper-lined tray; refrigerate 30 minutes.
7 Heat vegetable oil in deep medium saucepan; deep-fry fritters, in batches, until browned and heated through. Drain on absorbent paper.

prep + cook time 1 hour 30 minutes (+ refrigeration) **makes** 40
nutritional count per fritter 2.6g total fat (0.4g saturated fat); 196kJ (47 cal); 47.4g carbohydrate; 3.6g protein; 0.3g fibre
tip Salted cod, also known as salt cod, baccalà, bacalhau, bacalao and morue, is available from Italian, Spanish and Portuguese delicatessens and some speciality food stores. It needs to be de-salted and rehydrated before use.

Saffron and brandy squid

4 small cleaned squid hoods (300g), sliced thinly
2 cloves garlic, crushed
pinch saffron threads
2 teaspoons hot water
1 tablespoon olive oil
2 tablespoons brandy
100g (3 ounces) baby spinach leaves

1 Combine squid and garlic in medium bowl.
2 Place saffron in small dish; stir in the water.
3 Heat oil in large frying pan; cook squid until browned lightly, remove from pan.
4 Add brandy to pan; cook about 30 seconds or until brandy has almost evaporated.
5 Add spinach and saffron to pan; cook, stirring, until spinach wilts. Return squid to pan; season to taste, mix gently. Serve immediately.

prep + cook time 10 minutes **serves** 4
nutritional count per serving 5.6g total fat (1g saturated fat); 527kJ (126 cal); 0.3g carbohydrate; 13.2g protein; 0.9g fibre

Pan-seared scallops with anchovy butter

2 teaspoons olive oil
12 scallops (300g), roe removed
30g (1 ounce) butter
3 drained anchovy fillets
2 cloves garlic, crushed
2 teaspoons lemon juice
1 tablespoon finely chopped fresh chives

1 Heat oil in large frying pan; cook scallops, both sides, until browned lightly. Remove from pan; cover to keep warm.
2 Add butter, anchovies and garlic to pan; cook, stirring, until garlic is browned lightly. Return scallops to pan with juice; cook until scallops are heated through.
3 Serve scallops drizzled with anchovy butter and sprinkled with chives.

prep + cook time 15 minutes **serves** 4
nutritional count per serving 9.1g total fat (4.8g saturated fat); 514kJ (123 cal); 0.8g carbohydrate; 9.6g protein; 0.3g fibre

Octopus braised with red wine and fennel

1 tablespoon olive oil
1 medium brown onion (150g), chopped finely
2 cloves garlic, crushed
2 baby fennel bulbs (260g), trimmed, chopped coarsely
5 medium vine-ripened tomatoes (560g), chopped coarsely
3 dried bay leaves
1 teaspoon dried chilli flakes
680g (1¼ pounds) whole octopus
⅔ cup (160ml) dry red wine
2 tablespoons finely chopped fresh flat-leaf parsley

1 Preheat oven to 200°C/400°F.
2 Heat oil in large frying pan; cook onion and garlic, stirring, until onion softens. Add fennel; cook, stirring, 5 minutes. Add tomato, bay leaves and chilli; cook, stirring occasionally, about 10 minutes or until mixture thickens and fennel is softened.
3 Combine fennel mixture, octopus and wine in medium baking dish; bake, covered, about 45 minutes. Uncover; bake about 40 minutes or until octopus is tender and browned lightly.
4 Cut octopus into bite-sized pieces. Season to taste; stir in parsley. Serve with crusty bread, if you like.

prep + cook time 2 hours **serves** 8
nutritional count per serving 3g total fat (0.3g saturated fat);
493kJ (118 cal); 3.1g carbohydrate; 15.2g protein; 1.8g fibre

Potato, dill and prawn tortilla

30g (1 ounce) butter
2 teaspoons olive oil
2 medium potatoes (400g), chopped finely
1 medium brown onion (150g), chopped finely
12 uncooked medium king prawns (shrimp) (540g)
6 eggs
2 tablespoons sour cream
2 tablespoons finely chopped fresh dill

1 Preheat oven to 200°C/400°F.
2 Heat butter and oil in medium frying pan; cook potato, stirring occasionally, 5 minutes. Add onion; cook, stirring occasionally, until potato is browned and tender.
3 Meanwhile, shell and devein prawns, add to pan with potato; cook until prawns change colour.
4 Whisk eggs with sour cream in medium bowl until smooth; stir in dill, season. Pour mixture into pan; stir gently. Cook tortilla over low heat, about 10 minutes or until bottom sets. Wrap pan handle in foil; place pan in oven. Cook tortilla, uncovered, about 15 minutes or until tortilla is set and browned.
5 Stand tortilla 10 minutes before cutting into bite-sized pieces; serve warm.

prep + cook time 45 minutes **serves** 10
nutritional count per serving 8.3g total fat (3.8g saturated fat); 589kJ (141 cal); 5.5g carbohydrate; 10.7g protein; 0.8g fibre

Chicken, raisin and pine nut empanadas

1 litre (4 cups) water
1 chicken breast fillet (200g)
2 teaspoons olive oil
1 small brown onion (80g),
chopped finely
2 cloves garlic, crushed
200g (6½ ounces) canned
crushed tomatoes
1 dried bay leaf
¼ teaspoon dried chilli flakes
2 tablespoons raisins,
chopped coarsely

2 tablespoons pine nuts, roasted
½ teaspoon ground cinnamon
2 tablespoons finely chopped
fresh flat-leaf parsley
1 egg, beaten lightly
pastry
1⅔ cups (250g) plain
(all-purpose) flour
150g (4½ ounces) cold butter,
chopped
1 egg
1 tablespoon cold water

1 Bring the water to the boil in medium saucepan; add chicken, return to the boil. Reduce heat; simmer, covered, about 10 minutes or until chicken is cooked through. Cool chicken in poaching liquid 10 minutes. Remove chicken from pan; discard poaching liquid. Shred chicken finely.

2 Heat oil in medium frying pan; cook onion and garlic, stirring, until onion softens. Add undrained tomato, bay leaf and chilli; cook, stirring occasionally, about 5 minutes or until mixture thickens.

3 Add chicken, raisins, nuts and cinnamon to tomato mixture; stir until heated through. Season to taste; stir in parsley. Refrigerate, covered.

4 Meanwhile, make pastry.

5 Preheat oven to 200°C/400°F.

6 Roll one pastry half between sheets of baking paper until 2mm (⅛-inch) thick; cut ten 10cm (4-inch) rounds from pastry.

7 Place level tablespoon of chicken mixture in centre of each round; fold in half to enclose filling, pinch edges to seal. Seal edges of empanadas with a fork. Repeat with remaining pastry half and chicken mixture to make a total of 20 empanadas, re-rolling pastry scraps as required.

8 Place empanadas on baking-paper-lined oven trays; brush with egg. Bake about 20 minutes or until browned lightly.

pastry Process flour and butter until crumbly. Add egg and the water; process until mixture comes together. Knead dough on floured surface until smooth. Divide in half, enclose in plastic wrap; refrigerate 30 minutes.

prep + cook time 2 hours (+ refrigeration) **makes** 20
nutritional count per empanada 8.9g total fat (4.5g saturated fat); 594kJ (142 cal); 10.6g carbohydrate; 4.6g protein; 0.9g fibre

Lemon chilli chicken and chorizo skewers

400g (12½ ounces) chicken breast fillets,
    cut into 2cm (¾-inch) pieces
2 cured chorizo sausages (340g), cut into 2cm (¾-inch) pieces
1 medium yellow capsicum (bell pepper) (200g),
    cut into 2cm (¾-inch) pieces
12 fresh bay leaves
1 tablespoon finely grated lemon rind
1 tablespoon lemon juice
¼ cup (60ml) olive oil
2 cloves garlic, crushed
1 teaspoon dried chilli flakes
¼ cup finely chopped fresh flat-leaf parsley

1 Combine ingredients in large bowl; season. Cover; refrigerate 30 minutes.
2 Thread chicken, chorizo, capsicum and bay leaves, alternately,
onto skewers.
3 Cook skewers on heated oiled grill plate (or grill or barbecue) until
chicken is cooked through and chorizo is browned lightly.

prep + cook time 30 minutes (+ refrigeration) **makes** 12
nutritional count per skewer 15.3g total fat (4.4g saturated fat);
832kJ (199 cal); 1.3g carbohydrate; 14.3g protein; 0.4g fibre
tip Soak 12 bamboo skewers in water for at least an hour before using
to prevent them from scorching during cooking.

Sherry-glazed chicken livers

1 tablespoon olive oil
500g (1 pound) chicken livers, trimmed, sliced thinly
20g (¾ ounce) butter
2 shallots (50g), chopped finely
⅓ cup (80ml) dry sherry
½ cup (125ml) chicken stock
2 small long crusty bread rolls (120g), sliced into 6 slices each
30g (1 ounce) watercress sprigs
1 teaspoon sherry vinegar

1 Heat oil in large frying pan; add liver, stir over high heat about 1 minute or until liver is barely cooked. Remove from pan; cover to keep warm.
2 Add butter and shallot to same pan; cook, stirring, until shallot softens.
3 Add sherry to pan; simmer until liquid is reduced by half. Add stock; simmer until liquid is slightly thickened. Return liver to pan; stir until heated, season to taste.
4 Toast bread slices lightly both sides.
5 Spoon liver mixture over toast; sprinkle watercress with vinegar. Top toasts with watercress mixture.

prep + cook time 30 minutes **makes** 12
nutritional count per piece 4.9g total fat (1.7g saturated fat); 464kJ (111 cal); 6.1g carbohydrate; 8.7g protein; 0.5g fibre

de toros de 2

Fennel and garlic roasted pork ribs

1 tablespoon fennel seeds
⅓ cup (90g) tomato paste
1 tablespoon light brown sugar
¼ cup (60ml) sherry vinegar
4 cloves garlic, crushed
2 teaspoons smoked paprika
¼ cup (60ml) olive oil
2 x 500g (1-pound) racks american-style pork spareribs

1 Combine seeds, paste, sugar, vinegar, garlic, paprika and oil in medium jug. Reserve ¼ cup of marinade. Place pork in shallow dish, pour over marinade; turn pork to coat in marinade, season. Cover; refrigerate 1 hour.
2 Preheat oven to 200°C/400°F.
3 Place pork on oiled wire rack over large baking dish; roast, uncovered, 30 minutes.
4 Increase oven to 220°C/425°F. Brush pork with reserved marinade; roast about 20 minutes or until cooked through.
5 Cut ribs between the bones; serve with lemon wedges, if you like.

prep + cook time 1 hour (+ refrigeration) **serves** 6
nutritional count per serving 15.2g total fat (3.3g saturated fat); 915kJ (219 cal); 3.9g carbohydrate; 16.5g protein; 1g fibre

Artichoke and asparagus fritters with olive relish

170g (5½ ounces) asparagus, trimmed, chopped finely
280g (9 ounces) bottled artichokes in brine, drained, chopped finely
2 eggs
2 tablespoons finely chopped fresh mint
½ cup (40g) finely grated parmesan cheese
¼ cup (35g) self-raising flour
vegetable oil, for shallow-frying
olive relish
½ cup (60g) seeded green olives, chopped finely
½ cup (60g) seeded black olives, chopped finely
¼ cup finely chopped fresh flat-leaf parsley
1 tablespoon finely chopped fresh chives
1 tablespoon olive oil
1 tablespoon lemon juice

1 Make olive relish.
2 Combine asparagus, artichoke, eggs, mint, cheese and flour in medium bowl, season.
3 Heat oil in large frying pan; shallow-fry heaped tablespoons of fritter mixture, in batches, until browned all over and cooked through. Drain fritters on absorbent paper; serve hot with olive relish.
olive relish Combine ingredients in small bowl.

prep + cook time 40 minutes **makes** 15
nutritional count per fritter 4.6g total fat (1.2g saturated fat); 288kJ (69 cal); 3.8g carbohydrate; 2.9g protein; 0.8g fibre

Meatballs with gazpacho salsa

1 tablespoon olive oil
1 large brown onion (200g), chopped finely
2 cloves garlic, crushed
500g (1 pound) minced (ground) veal
2 tablespoons finely chopped fresh oregano
1½ cups (120g) finely grated manchego cheese
1 cup (70g) stale breadcrumbs
1 egg
vegetable oil, for shallow-frying
gazpacho salsa
1 lebanese cucumber (130g), seeded, chopped finely
1 medium green capsicum (bell pepper) (200g), chopped finely
½ small red onion (50g), chopped finely
1 small tomato (30g), seeded, chopped finely
2 tablespoons olive oil
1 tablespoon sherry vinegar

1 Make gazpacho salsa.
2 Heat olive oil in medium frying pan; cook onion and garlic, stirring, until onion softens. Cool 5 minutes.
3 Combine onion mixture, veal, oregano, cheese, breadcrumbs and egg in large bowl; season. Roll rounded tablespoons of mixture into balls.
4 Heat vegetable oil in large frying pan; shallow-fry meatballs, in batches, until cooked through. Drain on absorbent paper.
5 Serve meatballs hot with gazpacho salsa.
gazpacho salsa Combine ingredients in small bowl.

prep + cook time 50 minutes **makes** 40
nutritional count per meatball 4.1g total fat (1.1g saturated fat); 247kJ (59 cal); 1.7g carbohydrate; 3.7g protein; 0.3g fibre
tip Manchego cheese is a sharp, firm spanish cheese; it can be found in most specialty food stores and delicatessens. You can use parmesan cheese instead, if manchego is not available.

Roasted eggplant with marjoram vinaigrette

1 large eggplant (500g), sliced into 5mm (¼-inch) rounds
¼ cup (60ml) olive oil
1 small red onion (100g), sliced thinly
¼ cup (60ml) sherry vinegar
2 teaspoons caster (superfine) sugar
2 tablespoons finely chopped fresh marjoram
½ cup (125ml) olive oil, extra

1 Preheat oven to 200°C/400°F.
2 Brush both sides of eggplant slices with oil; place, in single layer, on baking-paper-lined oven trays. Roast about 25 minutes, turning eggplant slices once, until browned lightly both sides.
3 Meanwhile, combine onion, vinegar, sugar, marjoram and extra oil in small bowl; season to taste. Spoon onion mixture over eggplant.
4 Serve eggplant warm or at room temperature with crusty bread.

prep + cook time 50 minutes **serves** 6
nutritional count per serving 28.3g total fat (4g saturated fat); 1112kJ (278 cal); 4.6g carbohydrate; 1.2g protein; 2.2g fibre

Broad beans and thyme

600g (1¼ pounds) frozen broad beans (fava beans), thawed
10g (½ ounce) butter
2 shallots (50g), chopped finely
150g (4½ ounces) speck, chopped finely
1 tablespoon fresh thyme leaves
1 tablespoon lemon juice

1 Add beans to medium saucepan of boiling water, return to the boil; drain. When beans are cool enough to handle, peel away grey-coloured outer shells.
2 Heat butter in large frying pan; cook shallot and speck, stirring, until speck is browned lightly. Add beans and thyme; cook, stirring, until beans are heated through. Stir in juice; season to taste.

prep + cook time 40 minutes **serves** 4
nutritional count per serving 7.7g total fat (3.5g saturated fat); 589kJ (141 cal); 2g carbohydrate; 13.9g protein; 4.8g fibre

Chorizo and chickpeas in white wine

1 tablespoon olive oil
1 small brown onion (80g), sliced finely
2 cloves garlic, crushed
2 cured chorizo sausages (340g), chopped coarsely
1 medium red capsicum (bell pepper) (200g), sliced finely
400g (12½ ounces) canned chickpeas (garbanzo beans),
    rinsed, drained
½ teaspoon smoked paprika
¼ cup (60ml) dry white wine
⅓ cup (80ml) chicken stock

1 Heat oil in large frying pan; cook onion, garlic and chorizo, stirring,
until chorizo is browned lightly.
2 Add capsicum, chickpeas and paprika; cook, stirring, until capsicum is
tender. Add wine and stock; cook, stirring, until liquid is reduced by half.
Season to taste.

prep + cook time 25 minutes **serves** 6
nutritional count per serving 21.1g total fat (6.8g saturated fat);
1241kJ (297 cal); 9.6g carbohydrate; 14.6g protein; 3g fibre

Braised artichokes with crunchy almond topping

6 large globe artichokes (2.4kg)
4 dried bay leaves
4 cloves garlic
1 litre (4 cups) chicken stock
crunchy almond topping
¾ cup (50g) stale breadcrumbs
⅓ cup (25g) flaked almonds
2 tablespoons finely chopped fresh flat-leaf parsley
½ cup (60g) seeded green olives, chopped finely
¼ cup (60ml) olive oil
1 tablespoon finely grated lemon rind
2 tablespoons lemon juice

1 Preheat oven to 200°C/400°F.
2 Prepare artichokes by snapping off tough outer leaves and peeling stems. Trim stems to 5cm (2 inches). Cut 2cm (¾ inch) off top of artichokes to reveal chokes. Cut artichokes in half from top to bottom, then scoop out and discard furry chokes from centres. (As you finish preparing each artichoke, place it in a large bowl of water containing the juice of about half a lemon – this stops any discolouration while you are preparing the next one.)
3 Drain artichokes. Combine artichokes, bay leaves, garlic and stock in small baking dish, ensuring artichokes are covered with stock. Bake, covered, about 45 minutes or until artichokes are tender.
4 Meanwhile, make crunchy almond topping.
5 Drain artichokes; discard liquid.
6 Serve artichokes hot or at room temperature sprinkled with topping.
crunchy almond topping Combine breadcrumbs and nuts on oven tray; roast about 5 minutes or until browned lightly, cool 5 minutes. Combine breadcrumb mixture with remaining ingredients in small bowl.

prep + cook time 1 hour 40 minutes **serves** 6
nutritional count per serving 13.1g total fat (1.9g saturated fat); 928kJ (222 cal); 13.1g carbohydrate; 11.6g protein; 3.3g fibre

Roasted thyme potatoes with spicy sauce

500g (1 pound) baby new potatoes, halved
2 tablespoons olive oil
1 tablespoon finely chopped fresh thyme
spicy sauce
1 tablespoon olive oil
1 small brown onion (80g), chopped finely
2 cloves garlic, sliced thinly
1 fresh small red thai (serrano) chilli, chopped finely
400g (12½ ounces) canned crushed tomatoes
2 teaspoons caster (superfine) sugar

1 Preheat oven to 220°C/425°F.
2 Combine potatoes, oil and thyme in large baking dish; roast about
30 minutes or until potato is tender.
3 Meanwhile, make spicy sauce.
4 Serve spicy sauce with hot roasted potatoes.
spicy sauce Heat oil in medium saucepan; cook onion, garlic and chilli,
stirring, until onion softens. Add undrained tomatoes and sugar; bring
to the boil. Reduce heat; simmer, uncovered, stirring occasionally, about
10 minutes or until sauce thickens. Season to taste.

prep + cook time 45 minutes **serves** 8
nutritional count per serving 7g total fat (1g saturated fat);
506kJ (121 cal); 11.5g carbohydrate; 2.1g protein; 2.2g fibre

Rosemary potatoes with leek and chorizo

500g (1 pound) baby new potatoes, sliced thickly
2 cured chorizo sausages (340g), cut into 1cm (½-inch) thick slices
1 large leek (500g), trimmed, chopped coarsely
6 cloves garlic
1 tablespoon finely chopped fresh rosemary
2 teaspoons sweet paprika
5 dried bay leaves
¼ cup (60ml) olive oil

1 Preheat oven to 220°C/425°F.
2 Combine ingredients in large baking dish, season. Roast about
30 minutes or until potatoes are browned lightly.

prep + cook time 45 minutes **serves** 8
nutritional count per serving 19.8g total fat (5.6g saturated fat);
1120kJ (268 cal); 11g carbohydrate; 10.6g protein; 2.9g fibre

Smoked eggplant and capsicum jam

1 large eggplant (500g), chopped finely
1 medium red capsicum (bell pepper) (200g), chopped finely
1 medium red onion (170g), chopped finely
¼ cup (60ml) olive oil
1 tablespoon fresh thyme leaves
1 tablespoon smoked paprika
¼ teaspoon cayenne pepper
¼ cup (60ml) lemon juice
½ cup (125ml) water

1 Preheat oven to 220°C/425°F.
2 Combine eggplant, capsicum, onion and oil on baking-paper-lined oven tray; roast about 30 minutes or until vegetables are browned lightly.
3 Combine roasted vegetables, thyme, paprika, pepper, juice and the water in medium saucepan. Bring to the boil; reduce heat, simmer, uncovered, about 10 minutes or until jam is thickened. Season to taste.
4 Serve jam, warm or at room temperature, with char-grilled pitta bread.

prep + cook time 1 hour **serves** 8
nutritional count per serving 7.1g total fat (1g saturated fat); 364kJ (87 cal); 3.8g carbohydrate; 1.4g protein; 2g fibre
tip Smoked eggplant and capsicum jam can be tossed through pasta, spread on pizza bases, or served as side dish to chicken, lamb or fish.

Chunky olive and herb dip

½ cup (80g) finely chopped seeded green olives
½ cup each finely chopped fresh flat-leaf parsley and mint
¼ cup finely chopped fresh dill
6 drained anchovy fillets, chopped finely
2 teaspoons finely grated lemon rind
¼ cup (60ml) lemon juice
½ cup (125ml) olive oil

1 Combine ingredients in medium bowl; season to taste.

prep time 20 minutes **makes** 1½ cups
nutritional count per teaspoon 1.6g total fat (0.2g saturated fat);
67kJ (16 cal); 0.3g carbohydrate; 0.1g protein; 0.1g fibre
serving suggestions Crusty bread or crackers.

Pickled octopus

1.5kg (3-pound) large octopus
¾ cup (180ml) extra virgin olive oil
½ cup (125ml) white wine vinegar
1 clove garlic, crushed
2 tablespoons coarsely chopped fresh flat-leaf parsley

1 Clean octopus, remove eyes and beak. Place octopus in large
saucepan without any liquid. Cover pan, cook over low heat about 1 hour
or until octopus is tender. (The octopus will cook in its own juices but,
if necessary, add a little water if the juices evaporate.) Cool octopus in
pan until it is cool enough to handle. Rinse octopus under cold water,
remove skin, leaving tentacles intact.
2 Cut octopus into bite-sized pieces, place in medium bowl with
remaining ingredients; toss to combine. Cover; refrigerate overnight.
Serve sprinkled with parsley; accompany with lemon wedges, if you like.

prep + cook time 1 hour 10 minutes (+ cooling & refrigeration)
serves 8
nutritional count per serving 21.8g total fat (2.9g saturated fat);
1333kJ (319 cal); 0.2g carbohydrate; 30.8g protein; 0.1g fibre
tips We used large octopus in this recipe, but you could also use
baby octopus.
Recipe can be made up to four days ahead; store, covered, in refrigerator.

Sardines with caper and parsley topping

8 sardines (360g), cleaned
⅓ cup (50g) self-raising flour
½ teaspoon sweet paprika
olive oil, for shallow-frying
caper and parsley topping
2 tablespoons rinsed, drained baby capers, chopped finely
1 clove garlic, crushed
¼ cup finely chopped fresh flat-leaf parsley
2 teaspoons finely grated lemon rind
2 teaspoons lemon juice

1 Make caper and parsley topping.
2 To butterfly sardines, cut through the underside of the fish to the tail.
Break backbone at tail; peel away backbone. Trim sardines.
3 Coat fish in combined flour and paprika; shake away excess. Heat oil
in large frying pan; shallow-fry fish, in batches, until cooked through,
drain on absorbent paper.
4 Sprinkle fish with caper and parsley topping. Serve with lemon wedges,
if you like.
caper and parsley topping Combine ingredients in small bowl.

prep + cook time 45 minutes **serves** 8
nutritional count per serving 4.6g total fat (0.9g saturated fat);
376kJ (90 cal); 4.8g carbohydrate; 7.1g protein; 0.5g fibre
tip The caper and parsley topping is best made on the day of serving;
store, covered, in the refrigerator until ready to use.

Chorizo cones with chilli tomato salsa

450g (14½ ounces) canned refried beans
1 tablespoon water
2 cured chorizo sausages (340g), chopped finely
½ medium red capsicum (bell pepper) (100g), chopped finely
3 green onions (scallions), chopped finely
10 large (20cm/8-inch) flour tortillas, quartered
vegetable oil, for deep-frying
chilli tomato salsa
400g (12½ ounces) canned peeled tomatoes
2 fresh small red thai (serrano) chillies, seeded, quartered
1 clove garlic, quartered
⅓ cup loosely packed fresh coriander (cilantro) leaves
1 small brown onion (80g), quartered

1 Heat beans with the water in small saucepan.
2 Meanwhile, cook chorizo in large non-stick frying pan, stirring, until crisp; drain on absorbent paper.
3 Combine bean mixture and chorizo in medium bowl with capsicum and onion; season to taste. Divide filling among tortilla pieces; roll each tortilla around filling into cone shape, secure with toothpick.
4 Heat oil in large saucepan; deep-fry cones, in batches, until browned lightly and crisp. Drain on absorbent paper. Remove toothpicks.
5 Make chilli tomato salsa.
6 Serve hot cones with salsa.
chilli tomato salsa Blend or process ingredients until just combined.

prep + cook time 55 minutes **makes** 40
nutritional count per cone 4.9g total fat (1.3g saturated fat); 351kJ (84 cal); 6.5g carbohydrate; 3.2g protein; 1g fibre
tips Chorizo filling and chilli tomato salsa can be made a day ahead. Cover separately; refrigerate until required.
You need 40 toothpicks with points at each end for this recipe.

Chipotle beef on tortilla crisps

2 chipotle chillies (10g)
½ cup (125ml) boiling water
12 large (20cm/8-inch) white corn tortillas
vegetable oil, for deep-frying
1 tablespoon vegetable oil, extra
1 small brown onion (80g), sliced thinly
1 clove garlic, crushed
300g (9½ ounces) minced (ground) beef
1 tablespoon tomato paste
1 cup (250ml) beer
¼ cup coarsely chopped fresh coriander (cilantro)
½ cup (120g) sour cream

1 Cover chillies with the boiling water in small heatproof bowl; stand 20 minutes.
2 Meanwhile, cut three 7.5cm (3-inch) rounds from each tortilla. Heat oil in wok; deep-fry rounds, in batches, until browned lightly. Drain tortilla crisps on absorbent paper.
3 Drain chillies over small bowl; reserve liquid. Remove and discard stems from chillies. Blend or process chillies and reserved liquid until smooth.
4 Heat extra vegetable oil in medium frying pan; cook onion, stirring, until softened. Add garlic and beef; cook, stirring, until beef is browned. Stir in paste, beer and chilli puree; bring to the boil. Reduce heat; simmer, uncovered, about 15 minutes or until liquid is almost evaporated. Season to taste; stir in coriander.
5 Top each tortilla crisp with rounded teaspoon of beef mixture then with ½ teaspoon of sour cream.

prep + cook time 55 minutes (+ standing) **makes** 36
nutritional count per crisp 3.2g total fat (1.3g saturated fat); 238kJ (57 cal); 4.3g carbohydrate; 2.4g protein; 0.6g fibre

Prawns and tequila mayo on witlof leaves

900g (1¾ pounds) cooked medium king prawns (shrimp)
1 tablespoon tequila
¼ cup (75g) mayonnaise
1 tablespoon finely chopped fresh chives
3 red witlof (375g)

1 Shell and devein prawns. Chop prawn meat coarsely; combine in medium bowl with tequila, mayonnaise and chives. Season to taste.
2 Trim end from each witlof; separate leaves (you need 24 leaves). Place level tablespoon of prawn mixture on each leaf.

prep time 20 minutes **makes** 24
nutritional count per leaf 1.1g total fat (0.1g saturated fat); 130kJ (31 cal); 0.7g carbohydrate; 4g protein; 0.3g fibre

Gazpacho shooters with oysters

2 medium egg (plum) tomatoes (150g), chopped coarsely
1 small red capsicum (bell pepper) (150g), chopped coarsely
½ lebanese cucumber (65g), chopped coarsely
½ small red onion (50g), chopped coarsely
1 clove garlic, crushed
2 tablespoons olive oil
1 tablespoon white wine vinegar
1 cup (250ml) tomato juice
3 drops Tabasco sauce
½ teaspoon white (granulated) sugar
2 tablespoons water
24 oysters on the half shell

1 Blend or process tomato, capsicum, cucumber, onion, garlic, oil, vinegar, juice, sauce, sugar and the water until mixture is smooth. Push gazpacho through sieve into large jug; discard solids. Cover; refrigerate 2 hours. Season to taste.
2 Remove oysters from shells; discard shells. Divide gazpacho among 24 shot glasses; add one oyster to each.

prep time 15 minutes (+ refrigeration) **makes** 24
nutritional count per shot 1.8g total fat (0.3g saturated fat);
113kJ (27 cal); 1.2g carbohydrate; 1.5g protein; 0.3g fibre

Chorizo and potato fritters

2 teaspoons vegetable oil
1 cured chorizo sausage (170g), chopped finely
1 small brown onion (80g), chopped finely
2 fresh small red thai (serrano) chillies, chopped finely
2 medium zucchini (240g), grated coarsely
450g (14½ ounces) bintje potatoes, grated coarsely
1 small kumara (orange sweet potato) (250g), grated coarsely
3 eggs, beaten lightly
1 cup (150g) plain (all-purpose) flour
1 teaspoon sweet paprika
vegetable oil, for deep-frying
sweet chilli dipping sauce
½ cup (120g) sour cream
2 tablespoons sweet chilli sauce

1 Heat oil in medium frying pan; cook chorizo, onion and chilli, stirring, until onion softens. Add zucchini; cook, stirring, 1 minute. Cool 10 minutes.
2 Meanwhile, make sweet chilli dipping sauce.
3 Combine chorizo mixture in large bowl with potato, kumara, eggs, flour and paprika, season.
4 Heat oil in large saucepan; deep-fry level tablespoons of mixture, in batches, until fritters are browned lightly. Drain on absorbent paper. Serve with sweet chilli dipping sauce.
sweet chilli dipping sauce Combine ingredients in small bowl.

prep + cook time 40 minutes **makes** 40
nutritional count per fritter 4.6g total fat (1.1g saturated fat); 309kJ (74 cal); 5.3g carbohydrate; 2.6g protein; 0.6g fibre

Olive and cheese fritters

2 teaspoons (7g) dried yeast
1 cup (250ml) warm water
2 cups (300g) plain (all-purpose) flour
½ teaspoon salt
¼ cup (40g) seeded black olives, chopped coarsely
4 drained anchovy fillets, chopped finely
4 sun-dried tomatoes, drained, chopped finely
200g (6½ ounces) bocconcini cheese, chopped finely
1 small white onion (80g), chopped finely
2 cloves garlic, crushed
vegetable oil, for deep-frying

1 Combine yeast and the water in medium jug. Sift flour and salt into large bowl, gradually stir in yeast mixture to form a sticky, wet batter. Cover; stand in warm place about 1 hour or until doubled in size.
2 Stir olives, anchovy, tomato, cheese, onion and garlic into batter; season.
3 Heat oil in large saucepan; deep-fry heaped teaspoons of batter, in batches, about 3 minutes or until fritters are browned lightly and cooked through. Drain on absorbent paper; stand 2 minutes before serving.

prep + cook time 30 minutes (+ standing) **makes** 40
nutritional count per fritter 2.2g total fat (0.7g saturated fat); 213kJ (51 cal); 5.9g carbohydrate; 1.9g protein; 0.4g fibre

Saffron prawns

1kg (2 pounds) uncooked medium king prawns (shrimp)
1½ cups (225g) plain (all-purpose) flour
½ teaspoon salt
1½ cups (375ml) light beer
pinch saffron threads
vegetable oil, for deep-frying
1 medium lemon (140g), cut into wedges

1 Shell and devein prawns, leaving tails intact.
2 Sift flour and salt into large bowl; whisk in beer and saffron until smooth.
3 Heat oil in large saucepan. Pat prawns dry with absorbent paper.
Dip prawns in batter; drain off excess. Deep-fry prawns, in batches,
until changed in colour; drain on absorbent paper.
4 Serve immediately with lemon wedges.

prep + cook time 25 minutes **serves** 8
nutritional count per serving 8.3g total fat (1.1g saturated fat);
978kJ (234 cal); 21.3g carbohydrate; 16g protein; 1.1g fibre

Beef and almond empanadas

400g (12½ ounces) canned crushed tomatoes
1 tablespoon olive oil
1 medium brown onion (150g), chopped finely
1 clove garlic, crushed
1 teaspoon cracked black pepper
½ teaspoon each ground cinnamon and ground clove
600g (1¼ pounds) minced (ground) beef
¼ cup (40g) raisins, chopped coarsely
1 tablespoon cider vinegar
¼ cup (35g) slivered almonds, roasted
8 sheets shortcrust pastry
1 egg, beaten lightly
vegetable oil, for deep-frying

1 Blend or process undrained tomatoes until smooth; reserve.
2 Heat olive oil in large saucepan; cook onion, garlic and spices, stirring, until onion softens. Add beef; cook, stirring, until browned. Drain excess fat from pan. Stir in tomato, raisins and vinegar; simmer, uncovered, about 20 minutes or until mixture thickens. Season to taste; stir in nuts. Cool.
3 Cut 32 x 9cm (3¾-inch) rounds from pastry sheets. Place level tablespoon of beef mixture in centre of each round; brush edges with egg. Fold rounds in half to enclose filling; pinch edges to seal.
4 Heat vegetable oil in large saucepan; deep-fry empanadas, in batches, until crisp and browned lightly. Drain on absorbent paper. Serve immediately with a dollop of sour cream or bottled salsa, if desired.

prep + cook time 1 hour 30 minutes (+ cooling) **makes** 32
nutritional count per serving 18.9g total fat (7.5g saturated fat); 1166kJ (279 cal); 20.1g carbohydrate; 7g protein; 1.2g fibre

Fried oysters with salsa

1 small tomato (90g), chopped finely
½ medium yellow capsicum (bell pepper) (100g), chopped finely
½ medium red onion (85g), chopped finely
1 tablespoon finely chopped fresh coriander (cilantro)
1 tablespoon olive oil
1 tablespoon lime juice
1 fresh small red thai (serrano) chilli, seeded, chopped finely
12 oysters on the half shell
½ cup (85g) polenta
⅓ cup (80ml) milk
1 egg, beaten lightly
pinch cayenne pepper
vegetable oil, for deep-frying

1 Preheat oven to 180°C/350°F.
2 Combine tomato, capsicum, onion, coriander, olive oil, juice and
chilli in small bowl; season to taste.
3 Remove oysters from shells; reserve oysters. Place shells on oven tray;
heat in oven 5 minutes.
4 Meanwhile, combine polenta, milk, egg and pepper in small bowl.
5 Heat vegetable oil in medium saucepan. Dip oysters in batter;
deep-fry oysters, in batches, until browned lightly. Drain on absorbent
paper. Return oysters to shells; top with salsa.

prep + cook time 35 minutes **makes** 12
nutritional count per oyster 5.5g total fat (1g saturated fat);
276kJ (66 cal); 6.1g carbohydrate; 2.9g protein; 0.5g fibre

Crispy marinated whitebait

1kg (2 pounds) fresh or frozen whitebait
½ cup (125ml) red wine vinegar
4 cloves garlic, crushed
2 tablespoons finely chopped fresh oregano
1 fresh small red thai (serrano) chilli, chopped finely
1 teaspoon cracked black pepper
½ cup (75g) plain (all-purpose) flour
vegetable oil, for deep-frying
¼ cup loosely packed fresh oregano leaves

1 Combine whitebait, vinegar, garlic, oregano, chilli and pepper in large bowl. Cover; refrigerate 3 hours or overnight.
2 Drain the whitebait, pat dry with absorbent paper.
3 Toss whitebait and flour together in large bowl; season.
4 Heat vegetable oil in large saucepan; deep-fry oregano a few seconds or until crisp (be careful, oil may spit). Drain on absorbent paper.
5 Deep-fry whitebait, in batches, until browned lightly. Drain on absorbent paper. Serve topped with deep-fried oregano.

prep + cook time 25 minutes (+ refrigeration) **serves** 8
nutritional count per serving 23.7g total fat (4.8g saturated fat);
1409kJ (337 cal); 6.9g carbohydrate; 23.7g protein; 0.7g fibre

Pickled cauliflower, beetroot and turnip

3 cups (750ml) water
1½ cups (375ml) white wine vinegar
¼ cup (60g) fine sea salt
½ small cauliflower (500g), cut into florets
1 medium white turnip (230g), cut into wedges
8 baby beetroots (beets) (200g), unpeeled, cut into wedges
1 clove garlic, sliced thinly

1 Combine the water, vinegar and salt in medium saucepan; bring to
the boil. Boil, uncovered, 3 minutes.
2 Pack vegetables and garlic into hot sterilised 1.5-litre (6-cup) glass
jar with tight-fitting lid; pour in enough boiling vinegar mixture to cover
vegetables, leaving 1cm (½-inch) space between vegetables and top
of jar. Seal while hot. Store in cool, dark place for at least 3 days before
eating; once opened, store jar in refrigerator.

prep + cook time 20 minutes (+ standing) **makes** 4½ cups
nutritional count per ¼ cup 0g total fat (0g saturated fat);
67kJ (16 cal); 1.7g carbohydrate; 0.9g protein; 1g fibre

Soft shell crabs with green onion aïoli

½ cup (100g) rice flour
1 teaspoon dried chilli flakes
2 teaspoons sea salt flakes
8 uncooked small soft shell crabs (500g)
vegetable oil, for deep-frying
1 cup loosely packed fresh basil leaves
green onion aïoli
¾ cup (225g) mayonnaise
2 green onions (scallions), sliced thinly
1 clove garlic, crushed
1 tablespoon lemon juice

1 Make green onion aïoli.
2 Combine flour, chilli and salt in medium bowl.
3 Clean crabs; pat dry then cut into quarters. Coat crabs with flour mixture; shake off excess.
4 Heat oil in large saucepan; deep-fry basil about 30 seconds or until crisp. Drain on absorbent paper. Deep-fry crabs, in batches, until browned lightly. Drain on absorbent paper.
5 Serve crabs with basil, aïoli and lemon wedges, if you like.
green onion aïoli Combine ingredients in small bowl.

prep + cook time 30 minutes **serves** 8
nutritional count per serving 13g total fat (1.5g saturated fat); 920kJ (220 cal); 16.7g carbohydrate; 9g protein; 0.6g fibre
tip To clean the soft shell crabs, lift back the flap on undersides and wipe clean with a damp piece of absorbent paper. Never wash seafood under a running tap as this will wash away the "sea" flavour and waterlog the seafood. If you need to rinse, hold the seafood in one hand over the sink and use your other hand to gently splash the seafood with as little water as possible.

Sardine dip

180g (5½ ounces) light cream cheese, softened
2 tablespoons lemon juice
few drops Tabasco sauce
110g (3½ ounces) canned sardines in spring water, drained, mashed
1 shallot (25g), chopped finely
2 teaspoons finely chopped fresh flat-leaf parsley
¼ teaspoon cracked black pepper

1 Beat cream cheese, juice and sauce in small bowl with electric mixer until smooth.
2 Stir in remaining ingredients until combined; season to taste.

prep time 10 minutes **makes** 1 cup
nutritional count per tablespoon 11.7g total fat (6.6g saturated fat); 652kJ (156 cal); 2.4g carbohydrate; 10.3g protein; 0.2g fibre
tip Tabasco is the brand name of an extremely fiery sauce made from vinegar and red thai chillies. Use according to taste.
serving suggestion Sprinkle with extra finely chopped fresh flat-leaf parsley; serve with crusty bread or crackers.

Eggplant fritters

2 large eggplants (1kg)
1 cup (100g) coarsely grated mozzarella cheese
½ cup coarsely chopped fresh flat-leaf parsley
2 cloves garlic, crushed
½ cup (50g) packaged breadcrumbs
¼ cup (35g) plain (all-purpose) flour
2 eggs
vegetable oil, for shallow-frying

1 Preheat oven to 220°C/425°F.
2 Remove and discard stem ends from eggplants; prick eggplants all over with fork. Place on oiled oven tray; roast about 30 minutes or until soft. Cool. Peel eggplants; chop flesh finely.
3 Combine eggplant, cheese, parsley, garlic, breadcrumbs, flour and eggs in large bowl; season. Using wet hands, shape level tablespoons of mixture into oval patties.
4 Heat oil in large frying pan; shallow-fry fritters, in batches, until browned both sides. Drain on absorbent paper. Serve warm or cold.

prep + cook time 1 hour **makes** 36
nutritional count per fritter 5.3g total fat (1g saturated fat); 272kJ (65 cal); 2.4g carbohydrate; 1.7g protein; 0.8g fibre
serving suggestion Lemon wedges.

Spiced meatballs with romesco sauce

250g (8 ounces) cured chorizo sausages, chopped coarsely
1 small red onion (100g), chopped coarsely
2 cloves garlic, crushed
500g (1 pound) lean minced (ground) beef
½ teaspoon ground nutmeg
1 tablespoon dry sherry
½ cup (35g) stale breadcrumbs
olive oil, for shallow-frying
romesco sauce
1 teaspoon dried chilli flakes
2 cloves garlic, crushed
1 tablespoon slivered almonds, roasted
2 medium tomatoes (400g), chopped coarsely
¼ cup (60ml) extra virgin olive oil
1 tablespoon red wine vinegar

1 Make romesco sauce.
2 Blend or process chorizo, onion and garlic, pulsing until ingredients are finely chopped and combined. Transfer mixture to large bowl; stir in beef, nutmeg, sherry and breadcrumbs, season. Roll level tablespoons of mixture into balls.
3 Heat oil in large frying pan; shallow-fry meatballs, in batches, until browned and cooked through. Drain on absorbent paper.
4 Serve meatballs with romesco sauce.
romesco sauce Soak chilli flakes in hot water for 5 minutes; drain. Blend or process chilli, garlic, nuts and tomato until smooth. With motor operating, gradually add combined oil and vinegar in thin steady stream until sauce is smooth.

prep + cook time 40 minutes **makes** 40
nutritional count per meatball with sauce 6.7g total fat (1.6g saturated fat); 343kJ (82 cal); 1.1g carbohydrate; 4.1g protein; 0.3g fibre
tip Meatballs and sauce can be made a day ahead. To reheat the meatballs, place them in a single layer, on oven tray; cover with foil and make several slashes in the foil to allow steam to escape. Bake in oven preheated to 180°C/350°F for about 20 minutes.

Char-grilled banana chillies

4 red banana chillies (500g)
1 tablespoon white wine vinegar
1 tablespoon olive oil
2 teaspoons finely chopped fresh flat-leaf parsley

1 Preheat grill (broiler).
2 Cook whole chillies under hot grill until blistered and blackened.
Cover chillies with plastic or paper for 5 minutes; peel away skin.
3 Arrange whole chillies on serving plate; drizzle with combined vinegar,
oil and parsley. Season to taste.

prep + cook time 30 minutes **serves** 4
nutritional count per serving 4.8g total fat (0.6g saturated fat);
238kJ (57 cal); 2.1g carbohydrate; 0.8g protein; 1.4g fibre
tip Recipe can be made a day ahead; store, covered, in the refrigerator.

Orange-glazed squid

750g (1½ pounds) small squid hoods
3 cloves garlic, crushed
1 teaspoon sweet paprika
2 teaspoons finely grated orange rind
1 tablespoon orange juice
1 tablespoon red wine vinegar
¼ cup (55g) firmly packed light brown sugar
1 tablespoon olive oil
1 tablespoon finely chopped fresh coriander (cilantro)

1 Cut squid down centre to open out; cut into 5cm (2-inch) pieces.
2 Combine squid, garlic, paprika, rind, juice, vinegar, sugar and oil in medium bowl. Cover; refrigerate 3 hours or overnight.
3 Drain squid; reserve marinade. Cook squid in heated oiled large frying pan, in batches, until browned lightly and tender. Remove from pan.
4 Add reserved marinade to pan; bring to the boil. Reduce heat; simmer, uncovered, about 1 minute or until thickened slightly.
5 Combine squid and marinade mixture with coriander in large bowl; season to taste.

prep + cook time 30 minutes (+ refrigeration) **serves** 8
nutritional count per serving 3.4g total fat (0.7g saturated fat); 510kJ (122 cal); 7g carbohydrate; 15.8g protein; 0.2g fibre

Roasted mushroom salad

400g (12½ ounces) swiss brown mushrooms, halved
1 tablespoon fresh thyme leaves
2 cloves garlic, crushed
2 tablespoons sherry vinegar
½ cup (125ml) olive oil
3 cups (350g) firmly packed watercress sprigs

1 Preheat oven to 220°C/425°F.
2 Combine mushrooms, thyme, garlic, vinegar and oil in shallow medium baking dish, season.
3 Roast mushrooms, uncovered, about 20 minutes or until mushrooms are tender. Cool.
4 Combine mushrooms and their juice in large bowl with watercress.

prep + cook time 30 minutes **serves** 8
nutritional count per serving 14.4g total fat (2g saturated fat); 606kJ (145 cal); 0.9g carbohydrate; 2.3g protein; 1.9g fibre

Prawns with garlic herb butter

1kg (2 pounds) uncooked medium king prawns (shrimp)
2 tablespoons olive oil
6 cloves garlic, crushed
50g (1½ ounces) butter, chopped coarsely
1 tablespoon lemon juice
2 tablespoons finely chopped fresh flat-leaf parsley

1 Shell and devein prawns, leaving heads and tails intact.
2 Heat oil in large frying pan; cook garlic, stirring, until soft. Add prawns; cook, turning, until prawns start to change colour and are almost cooked. Add butter and juice; cook, turning, until prawns are cooked through. Stir in parsley.

prep + cook time 25 minutes **serves** 8
nutritional count per serving 10.1g total fat (4.1g saturated fat); 606kJ (145 cal); 0.3g carbohydrate; 13g protein; 0.4g fibre
serving suggestion Bread rolls and lemon wedges.

Fried chorizo with garlic

4 cured chorizo sausages (680g)
1 tablespoon olive oil
2 cloves garlic, crushed
¼ cup finely chopped fresh flat-leaf parsley

1 Cut chorizo into 5mm (¼-inch) slices.
2 Heat oil in large frying pan; cook chorizo, stirring, until crisp.
Add garlic; cook, stirring, 30 seconds. Remove from heat; stir in parsley.

prep + cook time 15 minutes **serves** 8
nutritional count per serving 27.8g total fat (9.6g saturated fat);
1350kJ (323 cal); 2.3g carbohydrate; 16.6g protein; 0.6g fibre

Paella croquettes

1 cup (200g) white long-grain rice
2 cups (500ml) chicken stock
1 dried bay leaf
1 teaspoon ground turmeric
2 teaspoons olive oil
1 clove garlic, crushed
1 medium red onion (170g), chopped coarsely
1 cured chorizo sausage (170g), chopped coarsely
100g (3 ounces) smoked chicken, chopped coarsely
1 tablespoon finely chopped fresh flat-leaf parsley
¼ cup (35g) plain (all-purpose) flour
2 eggs, beaten lightly
1 tablespoon milk
1 cup (100g) packaged breadcrumbs
vegetable oil, for deep-frying

1 Combine rice, stock, bay leaf and turmeric in medium saucepan; bring to the boil, stirring. Reduce heat; simmer, covered, about 12 minutes or until rice is tender. Remove from heat; stand, covered, 10 minutes. Fluff rice with fork, discard bay leaf; cool.
2 Meanwhile, heat olive oil in large frying pan; cook garlic, onion and chorizo, stirring, until onion softens; cool.
3 Blend or process rice, chorizo mixture, chicken and parsley until ingredients come together; season to taste. With wet hands, shape ¼ cups of rice mixture into croquettes. Toss croquettes in flour; shake off excess. Dip in combined eggs and milk, then in breadcrumbs. Place croquettes on baking-paper-lined tray; cover, refrigerate 30 minutes.
4 Heat vegetable oil in large saucepan; deep-fry croquettes, in batches, until browned lightly.

prep + cook time 50 minutes (+ cooling & refrigeration) **makes** 12
nutritional count per croquette 13.6g total fat (3.1g saturated fat); 1037kJ (248 cal); 22.3g carbohydrate; 9.2g protein; 0.9g fibre

Lamb and olive balls with anchovy aïoli

625g (1¼ pounds) minced (ground) lamb
1 medium red onion (170g), chopped finely
2 cloves garlic, chopped finely
4 drained anchovy fillets, chopped finely
2 teaspoons finely grated lemon rind
1 tablespoon finely chopped fresh thyme
2 tablespoons finely chopped fresh flat-leaf parsley
30 large pimiento-stuffed green olives (150g)
½ cup (75g) plain (all-purpose) flour
2 eggs, beaten lightly
2 cups (340g) polenta
vegetable oil, for shallow-frying
anchovy aïoli
2 egg yolks
2 drained anchovy fillets
1 clove garlic, chopped coarsely
1 teaspoon finely grated lemon rind
1 tablespoon lemon juice
¾ cup (180ml) olive oil

1 Combine lamb, onion, garlic, anchovy, rind and herbs in large bowl;
season. Roll level tablespoon of mixture into a ball around each olive;
place on tray. Refrigerate 1 hour.
2 Meanwhile, make anchovy aïoli.
3 Toss balls in flour; shake off excess. Dip balls in egg, then roll in
polenta; place on tray. Refrigerate 1 hour.
4 Heat oil in medium frying pan; shallow-fry meatballs, in batches,
until browned and cooked. Drain on absorbent paper.
5 Serve meatballs with aïoli and lemon wedges.
anchovy aïoli Blend or process egg yolks, anchovy, garlic, rind and
juice until smooth. With motor operating, gradually add oil in thin steady
stream; blend until thick. Drizzle with extra olive oil to serve.

prep + cook time 50 minutes (+ refrigeration) **makes** 30
nutritional count per ball 13.9g total fat (2.7g saturated fat);
815kJ (195 cal); 11.1g carbohydrate; 6.4g protein; 0.6g fibre
tip For a quick version of anchovy aïoli, stir finely chopped anchovies,
garlic, lemon rind and juice into your favourite mayonnaise.

Pork, olive and egg empanadas

1 tablespoon olive oil
1 medium brown onion (150g), chopped finely
½ teaspoon each ground cumin, cinnamon and smoked paprika
¼ teaspoon each ground nutmeg and cloves
375g (12 ounces) minced (ground) pork
2 hard-boiled eggs, grated coarsely
⅓ cup (40g) seeded black olives, chopped finely
6 sheets shortcrust pastry
1 egg, beaten lightly

1 Heat oil in large frying pan; cook onion, stirring, until soft. Add spices and pork; cook, stirring, until browned. Cool.
2 Stir hard-boiled eggs and olives into pork mixture; season.
3 Preheat oven to 200°C/400°F. Oil two oven trays.
4 Cut 24 x 12cm (5-inch) rounds from pastry. Place heaped tablespoon of pork mixture in centre of each round; brush edges with egg. Fold rounds in half to enclose filling; pinch edges to seal.
5 Place empanadas on oven trays with sealed edge upright; brush with egg. Bake about 25 minutes or until browned lightly.

prep + cook time 1 hour **makes** 24
nutritional count per empanada 14g total fat (6.7g saturated fat); 961kJ (230 cal); 19.2g carbohydrate; 6.7g protein; 0.9g fibre
serving suggestion Lemon wedges and black olives.

Snails with green sauce

1 tablespoon olive oil
1 small brown onion (80g), chopped finely
4 cloves garlic, crushed
1 teaspoon plain (all-purpose) flour
2 tablespoons dry white wine
¼ cup (60ml) fish stock
2 tablespoons pouring cream
¼ cup finely chopped fresh flat-leaf parsley
24 large fresh or canned snails with shells, drained

1 Preheat oven to 220°C/425°F.
2 Heat oil in small saucepan; cook onion and garlic, stirring, until onion softens. Add flour; cook, stirring, until mixture bubbles and thickens. Gradually stir in combined wine, stock and cream; cook, stirring, until sauce boils and thickens. Season to taste; stir in parsley.
3 Meanwhile, push the snails into shells. Arrange snails on oven tray; bake about 5 minutes or until heated through.
4 Serve snails with sauce.

prep + cook time 25 minutes **makes** 24
nutritional count per snail 1.7g total fat (0.6g saturated fat); 113kJ (27 cal); 1.1g carbohydrate; 1.7g protein; 0.1g fibre
tip You will need the snails' shells for this recipe.

Roast potatoes with aïoli

1kg (2 pounds) baby new potatoes, quartered
2 tablespoons olive oil
¼ teaspoon hot paprika
aïoli
2 egg yolks
3 cloves garlic, quartered
¾ cup (180ml) olive oil

1 Preheat oven to 240°C/475°F.
2 Combine potatoes and oil in large baking dish. Roast about 40 minutes or until potatoes are browned and crisp.
3 Meanwhile, make aïoli.
4 Sprinkle aïoli with paprika and serve with potatoes.
aïoli Blend or process egg yolks and garlic until smooth. With motor operating, gradually add oil in thin steady stream; process until thick. Season to taste.

prep + cook time 50 minutes **serves** 10
nutritional count per serving 21.3g total fat (3.2g saturated fat); 1091kJ (261 cal); 13.4g carbohydrate; 3.1g protein; 2.3g fibre
tips The aïoli can be made a day ahead; store, covered, in the refrigerator. Add a little lemon juice to the aïoli, to taste, if you like.

Crumbed sardines
with roasted tomato sauce

24 butterflied sardines (1kg)
¼ cup (35g) plain (all-purpose) flour
4 eggs, beaten lightly
3½ cups (245g) stale breadcrumbs
½ cup finely chopped fresh flat-leaf parsley
¼ cup finely chopped fresh oregano
vegetable oil, for deep-frying
roasted tomato sauce
6 medium egg (plum) tomatoes (450g), chopped coarsely
4 cloves garlic, peeled
2 tablespoons red wine vinegar
2 tablespoons light brown sugar
1 large brown onion (200g), chopped coarsely
2 tablespoons olive oil

1 Make roasted tomato sauce.
2 Meanwhile, coat sardines in flour; shake off excess. Dip sardines in egg, then in combined breadcrumbs and herbs.
3 Heat oil in large saucepan; deep-fry sardines, in batches, until browned and cooked through. Drain on absorbent paper.
4 Serve sardines with sauce.
roasted tomato sauce Preheat oven to 220°C/425°F. Combine ingredients in large baking dish. Bake about 30 minutes or until onion softens. Blend or process tomato mixture until smooth; season to taste.

prep + cook time 40 minutes **serves** 6
nutritional count per serving 42.9g total fat (8.7g saturated fat); 3097kJ (741 cal); 38.8g carbohydrate; 48.4g protein; 3.8g fibre
serving suggestion Lemon wedges.

Spiced pork skewers with orange honey glaze

500g (1 pound) pork fillet
2 cloves garlic, crushed
2 teaspoons cumin seeds
½ teaspoon ground coriander
¼ teaspoon sweet paprika
1 tablespoon olive oil
orange honey glaze
½ cup (125ml) orange juice
2 tablespoons honey
2 tablespoons barbecue sauce
1 teaspoon dijon mustard

1 Cut pork into 2.5cm (1-inch) pieces. Combine pork, garlic, seeds, spices and oil in medium bowl; season.
2 Thread pork onto eight bamboo skewers.
3 Cook skewers on heated oiled grill plate (or grill or barbecue) until browned and cooked through.
4 Meanwhile, make orange honey glaze.
5 Serve skewers with glaze.
orange honey glaze Stir ingredients in small saucepan over heat until boiling. Reduce heat; simmer, uncovered, about 5 minutes or until thickened.

prep + cook time 30 minutes **makes** 8
nutritional count per skewer 3.8g total fat (0.8g saturated fat); 535kJ (128 cal); 9.7g carbohydrate; 13.9g protein; 0.2g fibre
tip Soak skewers in water for at least 1 hour before using, to avoid scorching during cooking.

Blood orange and chilli glazed quail

6 quails (960g)
1 teaspoon cumin seeds
½ cup (125ml) blood orange juice
1 fresh long red chilli, chopped finely
1 clove garlic, crushed
2 tablespoons light brown sugar
1 tablespoon finely chopped fresh coriander (cilantro)

1 Using kitchen scissors, cut along both sides of quails' backbones; discard backbones. Halve each quail along breastbone; cut each in half again to give a total of 24 pieces.
2 Cook quail, covered, on heated oiled grill plate (or grill or barbecue) about 20 minutes or until cooked through.
3 Meanwhile, dry-fry seeds in small saucepan until fragrant. Add juice, chilli, garlic and sugar; stir over heat, without boiling, until sugar dissolves. Bring to the boil; boil, uncovered, about 5 minutes or until mixture is thick and syrupy.
4 Combine hot quail, syrup and coriander in large bowl.

prep + cook time 35 minutes **serves** 8
nutritional count per serving 6.6g total fat (1.7g saturated fat); 514kJ (123 cal); 4.4g carbohydrate; 11.3g protein; 0.1g fibre

Seafood

Spicy sardines with orange and olive salad

24 butterflied sardines (1kg)
1 clove garlic, crushed
1 tablespoon olive oil
2 tablespoons orange juice
1 teaspoon hot paprika
1 teaspoon finely chopped fresh oregano
orange and olive salad
2 medium oranges (480g)
⅓ cup (40g) seeded black olives, chopped coarsely
50g (1½ ounces) baby rocket leaves (arugula)
1 fresh long red chilli, sliced thinly
1 tablespoon orange juice
½ teaspoon finely chopped fresh oregano
1 tablespoon olive oil

1 Combine ingredients in medium bowl; season.
2 Make orange and olive salad.
3 Cook sardines, in batches, on heated oiled grill plate (or grill or barbecue) until browned both sides and cooked through.
4 Divide sardines among plates; serve with salad.
orange and olive salad Peel then segment oranges over medium bowl; add remaining ingredients, toss gently to combine.

prep + cook time 35 minutes **serves** 4
nutritional count per serving 36.2g total fat (8.3g saturated fat); 2500kJ (598 cal); 11.5g carbohydrate; 56g protein; 2.2g fibre
tip Sardines are available already butterflied from most fishmongers.

Ceviche

1kg (2 pounds) skinless redfish fillets
1½ cups (375ml) lime juice
¼ cup (40g) canned jalapeño chilli slices, drained
¼ cup (60ml) olive oil
1 large tomato (250g), chopped coarsely
¼ cup finely chopped fresh coriander (cilantro)
1 small white onion (80g), chopped finely
1 clove garlic, crushed

1 Remove any remaining skin or bones from fish; cut fish into 2.5cm (1-inch) pieces.
2 Combine fish and juice in non-reactive large bowl; cover, refrigerate overnight.
3 Drain fish; discard juice. Return fish to bowl, add remaining ingredients; toss gently to combine. Cover; refrigerate 1 hour. Season to taste.

prep time 15 minutes (+ refrigeration) **serves** 4
nutritional count per serving 18.5g total fat (3.4g saturated fat); 1685kJ (403 cal); 3.7g carbohydrate; 52.8g protein; 1.6g fibre
tips You will need about 10 limes for this recipe.
The lime juice "cooks" the fish. Fish must be marinated with the lime juice in a non-reactive bowl (one made from glazed porcelain or glass is best), to avoid the metallic taste that can result if marinating takes place in a stainless-steel or an aluminium bowl. Ensure all of the fish is completely covered with juice.

Squid, chorizo and tomato salad

900g (1¾ pounds) squid hoods
2 cured chorizo sausages (340g), sliced thinly
1 tablespoon olive oil
4 medium tomatoes (600g), seeded, sliced thickly
1.2kg (2½ pounds) canned white beans, rinsed, drained
2 cups loosely packed fresh flat-leaf parsley leaves
1 teaspoon finely grated lemon rind
¼ cup (60ml) lemon juice

1 Cut squid down centre to open out; score the inside in diagonal pattern then cut into 2cm (¾-inch) strips.
2 Cook chorizo in heated large frying pan, stirring, until browned. Remove from pan.
3 Cook squid, in batches, in same pan until tender.
4 Place chorizo and squid in large bowl with remaining ingredients; toss gently to combine. Season to taste.

prep + cook time 45 minutes **serves** 4
nutritional count per serving 33.3g total fat (11g saturated fat); 2449kJ (586 cal); 8.5g carbohydrate; 59.9g protein; 6.5g fibre
tip Many varieties of already cooked white beans are available canned, among them cannellini, butter and haricot beans; any of these are suitable for this salad.

Garlic prawns

1 ¼ cups (310ml) olive oil
¾ cup (180ml) dry white wine
2 tablespoons lemon juice
6 cloves garlic, sliced thinly
1 fresh long red chilli, chopped finely
1kg (2 pounds) uncooked large king prawns (shrimp)
⅓ cup coarsely chopped fresh flat-leaf parsley

1 Preheat oven to 220°C/425°F.
2 Stir oil, wine, juice, garlic and chilli in large flameproof baking dish over low heat 5 minutes or until fragrant. Cool 15 minutes.
3 Meanwhile, shell and devein prawns, leaving tails intact.
4 Add prawns to oil mixture; mix well. Transfer to oven; cook 10 minutes or until prawns change colour. Season to taste.
5 Spoon prawn mixture in shallow bowls; sprinkle with parsley.

prep + cook time 45 minutes (+ cooling) **serves** 4
nutritional count per serving 71.4g total fat (10.1g saturated fat); 3227kJ (772 cal); 0.9g carbohydrate; 26.2g protein; 1g fibre
serving suggestion Crusty bread to soak up the juices.

Seafood paella with aïoli

500g (1 pound) clams
½ teaspoon saffron threads
2 tablespoons boiling water
¼ cup (60ml) olive oil
1 large brown onion (200g),
 chopped finely
4 cloves garlic, crushed
4 medium tomatoes (600g)
 chopped finely
1 teaspoon white (granulated)
 sugar
800g (1½ pounds) uncooked
 medium king prawns (shrimp)

2 teaspoons sweet paprika
1 litre (4 cups) water
2 cups (400g) white short-grain rice
400g (12½ ounces) skinless
 white fish fillets, cut into
 4cm (1½-inch) pieces
1 cup (120g) frozen peas
⅓ cup coarsely chopped fresh
 flat-leaf parsley

aïoli
1 cup (300g) mayonnaise
2 tablespoons lemon juice
2 cloves garlic, crushed

1 Rinse clams under cold water; place in large bowl of cold salted water, stand 2 hours. Discard water then rinse clams thoroughly; drain.
2 Combine saffron and the boiling water in small heatproof bowl.
3 Heat oil in 40cm (16-inch) round shallow frying pan; cook onion over medium heat, stirring, about 10 minutes or until soft and golden brown. Add garlic; cook, stirring, 1 minute. Add tomato; cook, stirring frequently, about 15 minutes or until pulpy. Stir in sugar.
4 Meanwhile, shell and devein prawns, leaving tails intact.
5 Stir saffron mixture, paprika, the water and rice into pan; bring to the boil. Reduce heat, place clams, prawns and fish on top of rice (do not stir to combine); simmer, uncovered, without stirring, about 20 minutes or until rice is almost tender. Sprinkle peas into pan; simmer, uncovered, about 3 minutes or until liquid is absorbed. Remove pan from heat, cover; stand 10 minutes. Season to taste; stir in parsley.
6 Meanwhile, make aïoli. Serve paella with aïoli.
aïoli Combine ingredients in small serving bowl.

prep + cook time 1 hour (+ standing) **serves** 6
nutritional count per serving 28.2g total fat (4g saturated fat); 2897kJ (693 cal); 68.9g carbohydrate; 38.2g protein; 4.3g fibre
tips Calasparra or bomba are the correct Spanish rices to use for paella, but arborio rice will do just as well.
If you're short on time, some fish markets sell prepared clams, shelled prawns and chopped chunks of fish.

Cuttlefish with saffron rice

600g (1¼ pounds) cuttlefish hoods
2 tablespoons olive oil
1 medium red onion (170g), sliced thinly
2 cloves garlic, sliced thinly
1½ cups (300g) white short-grain rice
1 tablespoon tomato paste
1 teaspoon sweet paprika
pinch saffron threads
½ cup (125ml) dry white wine
1 litre (4 cups) chicken stock
1 cup (250ml) water
4 medium tomatoes (600g), seeded, sliced thickly
½ cup coarsely chopped fresh flat-leaf parsley

1 Cut cuttlefish down centre to open out; score inside in a diagonal pattern. Cut cuttlefish, lengthways, into three pieces.
2 Heat half the oil in large deep frying pan; cook onion and garlic, stirring, until onion is soft. Stir in rice, paste, paprika and saffron. Add wine; cook, stirring, until liquid is almost evaporated. Stir in stock and the water; bring to the boil. Reduce heat; simmer, uncovered, until rice is tender and liquid is almost evaporated. Season to taste.
3 Meanwhile, heat remaining oil in large frying pan; cook cuttlefish, stirring, until cuttlefish changes colour. Remove from heat, stir in tomato and parsley.
4 Serve rice topped with cuttlefish mixture. Serve with lemon wedges, if you like.

prep + cook time 30 minutes **serves** 4
nutritional count per serving 12.6g total fat (2.5g saturated fat); 2316kJ (554 cal); 67g carbohydrate; 35.4g protein; 3.8g fibre
tip Calasparra or bomba are the correct Spanish rices to use for paella, but arborio rice will do just as well.

Sardines with tomatoes and caper dressing

12 whole sardines (540g), cleaned
4 medium egg (plum) tomatoes (300g), sliced thickly
1 small red onion (100g), sliced thinly
caper dressing
⅓ cup (80ml) red wine vinegar
¼ cup (60ml) olive oil
1 tablespoon drained, rinsed baby capers
1 clove garlic, crushed
2 tablespoons coarsely chopped fresh flat-leaf parsley

1 Remove and discard sardine heads. To butterfly sardines, cut through the underside of fish to the tail. Break backbone at tail; peel away backbone. Trim sardines.
2 Cook sardines on heated oiled grill plate (or grill or barbecue) until browned both sides and cooked.
3 Meanwhile, make caper dressing.
4 Serve sardines with tomato and onion; drizzle with dressing.
caper dressing Place ingredients in screw-top jar; shake well. Season to taste.

prep + cook time 35 minutes **serves** 4
nutritional count per serving 16.3g total fat (2.7g saturated fat); 1091kJ (261 cal); 3.2g carbohydrate; 24.2g protein; 1.5g fibre
serving suggestion Crusty bread.

Seafood risoni paella

12 uncooked medium king prawns (shrimp) (540g)
250g (8 ounces) small mussels
300g (9½ ounces) white fish fillets, cut into 2.5cm (1-inch) pieces
2 tablespoons olive oil
1 small brown onion (80g), chopped finely
4 cloves garlic, crushed
500g (1 pound) risoni
pinch saffron threads
1 cup (250ml) dry white wine
6 small tomatoes (780g), seeded, chopped coarsely
2 tablespoons tomato paste
1 teaspoon finely grated orange rind
4 sprigs fresh marjoram
1 litre (4 cups) vegetable stock, warmed
1½ cups (185g) frozen peas
150g (4½ ounces) calamari rings

1 Shell and devein prawns, leaving tails intact. Scrub mussels; remove beards.
2 Heat oil in large deep frying pan; cook onion and garlic, stirring, until onion softens. Add risoni and saffron; stir to coat in onion mixture. Stir in wine, tomato, paste, rind and marjoram; cook, stirring, until wine has almost evaporated.
3 Add 1 cup of the stock, stirring, until absorbed. Add remaining stock; cook, stirring, until risoni is almost tender.
4 Place peas and seafood on top of risoni mixture (do not stir to combine); cover pan. Reduce heat; simmer 10 minutes or until seafood has changed colour and mussels opened (discard any that do not). Season to taste.

prep + cook time 1 hour **serves** 4
nutritional count per serving 14.6g total fat (2.9g saturated fat); 3394kJ (812 cal); 95.6g carbohydrate; 58.1g protein; 9g fibre
tips While paella is traditionally made with short-grain white rice, risoni makes an interesting alternative. This tiny short pasta adds a smoother texture to the finished dish.
This recipe can be made in a traditional paella pan if you own one; otherwise a deep frying pan or wok with a tight-fitting lid will suffice. Serve the paella straight from the pan at the table.
We used ling in this recipe but you can use any white fish fillets you like.

Octopus braised in red wine

⅓ cup (80ml) olive oil
600g (1¼ pounds) baby onions, halved
4 cloves garlic, crushed
1.5kg (3 pounds) cleaned baby octopus, halved
1½ cups (375ml) dry red wine
⅓ cup (95g) tomato paste
⅓ cup (80ml) red wine vinegar
3 large tomatoes (660g), peeled, seeded, chopped coarsely
2 dried bay leaves
1 fresh long red chilli, chopped finely
10 drained anchovy fillets (30g), chopped coarsely
⅓ cup finely chopped fresh oregano
1 cup coarsely chopped fresh flat-leaf parsley

1 Heat oil in large saucepan; cook onion and garlic, stirring, until onion softens. Add octopus; cook, stirring, until just changed in colour.
2 Add wine; cook, stirring, about 5 minutes or until liquid is reduced by about a third. Add paste, vinegar, tomato, bay leaves, chilli and anchovy; bring to the boil. Reduce heat; simmer, covered, 1 hour. Uncover; simmer about 30 minutes or until sauce thickens and octopus is tender.
3 Remove pan from heat; season to taste. Stir in oregano and parsley.

prep + cook time 2 hours **serves** 6
nutritional count per serving 17.2g total fat (2.8g saturated fat); 2169kJ (519 cal); 10.2g carbohydrate; 67.9g protein; 3.2g fibre
tip Ask your fishmonger to clean the octopus and remove the beaks.
serving suggestion Thick slices of toasted bread to soak up the juices.

Garlic prawns with citrus salad

20 uncooked large king prawns (shrimp) (1.4kg)
3 cloves garlic, crushed
2 teaspoons finely grated lime rind
⅓ cup (80ml) lime juice
2 tablespoons olive oil
2 lebanese cucumbers (260g), sliced thinly
250g (8 ounces) cherry tomatoes, halved
1 cup (150g) seeded black olives
3 small oranges (540g), segmented
1 medium red onion (170g), halved, sliced thickly
400g (12½ ounces) baby curly endive, trimmed, torn
lime and orange dressing
2 teaspoons finely grated lime rind
¼ cup (60ml) lime juice
¼ cup (60ml) orange juice
1 tablespoon olive oil

1 Shell and devein prawns, leaving tails intact.
2 Place prawns in medium bowl with garlic, rind, juice and oil; toss gently to combine. Cover; refrigerate 3 hours or overnight, turning occasionally.
3 Cook drained prawns on heated oiled grill plate (or grill or barbecue) until changed in colour.
4 Meanwhile, make lime and orange dressing.
5 Place prawns in large bowl with cucumber, tomato, olives, orange, onion and dressing; toss gently to combine. Season to taste.
6 Divide endive among serving plates; top with salad.
lime and orange dressing Place ingredients in screw-top jar; shake well.

prep + cook time 40 minutes (+ refrigeration) **serves** 4
nutritional count per serving 15.7g total fat (2.2g saturated fat);
1743kJ (417 cal); 23.3g carbohydrate; 40.4g protein; 7.5g fibre

Baked fish with saffron, leek and potato

2 tablespoons olive oil
600g (1¼ pounds) kipfler potatoes, sliced thickly
2 medium leeks (700g), sliced thickly
4 cloves garlic, bruised
pinch saffron threads
2 cups (500ml) chicken stock
4 x 200g (6½-ounce) white fish fillets

1 Preheat oven to 220°C/425°F.
2 Heat oil in large flameproof baking dish; cook potato, leek and garlic, stirring, until leek softens. Add saffron and stock; bring to the boil. Reduce heat; simmer, uncovered, 10 minutes.
3 Add fish, cover, transfer to oven; bake 20 minutes or until cooked through. Season to taste.
4 Serve fish topped with potato and leek; drizzle with pan juices.

prep + cook time 35 minutes **serves** 4
nutritional count per serving 14.6g total fat (3g saturated fat); 1831kJ (438 cal); 24.9g carbohydrate; 48.1g protein; 6.6g fibre
tip We used blue-eye in this recipe but you can use any white fish fillets you like.
serving suggestion Sprinkle with fresh chervil leaves.

Olive and anchovy-stuffed garfish

500g (1 pound) truss cherry tomatoes
½ cup (75g) fetta-stuffed green olives, chopped finely
2 tablespoons finely chopped fresh flat-leaf parsley
2 drained anchovy fillets, chopped finely
1 clove garlic, crushed
¼ cup (60ml) olive oil
8 cleaned whole garfish (750g), butterflied
1 medium red onion (170g), sliced thinly
2 tablespoons red wine vinegar
1 cup firmly packed fresh basil leaves, torn
2 tablespoons plain (all-purpose) flour

1 Preheat oven to 220°C/425°F.
2 Place tomatoes on oiled oven tray; roast 10 minutes or until softened.
3 Meanwhile, combine olives, parsley, anchovy, garlic and 1 tablespoon of the oil in medium bowl; season to taste. Fill cavities of garfish with olive mixture; secure with kitchen string.
4 Combine onion and vinegar in small bowl; stand 10 minutes. Add basil; mix gently.
5 Coat garfish in flour; shake off excess. Heat remaining oil in large frying pan; cook garfish until browned both sides and cooked through.
6 Serve garfish with tomato and basil salad.

prep + cook time 40 minutes **serves** 4
nutritional count per serving 16.8g total fat (2.6g saturated fat); 1216kJ (291 cal); 9.6g carbohydrate; 23.2g protein; 4.8g fibre

Prawn cantinas

18 uncooked medium king prawns (shrimp) (810g)
2 tablespoons lemon juice
1 tablespoon olive oil
1 teaspoon sweet smoked paprika
6 baps or other small bread rolls
120g (4 ounces) baby rocket leaves (arugula)
buttermilk aïoli
⅓ cup (80ml) buttermilk
1 tablespoon mayonnaise
2 cloves garlic, crushed

1 Shell and devein prawns. Combine prawns, juice, oil and paprika in medium bowl; season.
2 Make buttermilk aïoli.
3 Cook prawn mixture in heated large frying pan, stirring, about 3 minutes or until prawns change colour.
4 Cut slits in top of rolls. Combine rocket and aïoli, divide among rolls; top with warm prawn mixture.
buttermilk aïoli Combine ingredients in small bowl.

prep + cook time 15 minutes **makes** 6
nutritional count per roll 6.1g total fat (1g saturated fat);
844kJ (202 cal); 18g carbohydrate; 17.8g protein; 1.6g fibre

Prawns with wine and tomato

1kg (2 pounds) uncooked medium tiger prawns (shrimp)
2 tablespoons olive oil
8 green onions (scallions), sliced thinly
4 cloves garlic, sliced thinly
½ cup (125ml) dry white wine
2⅔ cups (700g) bottled tomato pasta sauce
2 tablespoons coarsely chopped fresh oregano leaves

1 Shell and devein prawns, leaving tails intact.
2 Heat oil in large frying pan; cook prawns, onion and garlic, in two batches, until prawns change colour. Transfer to large bowl.
3 Add wine to same heated pan; simmer, uncovered, until liquid is reduced by half. Add pasta sauce; bring to the boil. Reduce heat; simmer, uncovered, about 5 minutes or until sauce thickens.
4 Add prawn mixture and oregano to pan, season to taste; stir gently until heated through.

prep + cook time 30 minutes **serves** 4
nutritional count per serving 3.1g total fat (0.4g saturated fat); 364kJ (87 cal); 5g carbohydrate; 7.8g protein; 1.1g fibre
serving suggestion Risoni pasta.

Spicy squid with olives

2 tablespoons olive oil
1 medium red onion (170g), chopped finely
3 cloves garlic, crushed
2 fresh small red thai (serrano) chillies, sliced thinly
½ cup (125ml) dry white wine
800g (1½ pounds) canned cherry tomatoes
¾ cup (180ml) water
800g (1½ pounds) baby squid with tentacles
1 cup (160g) seeded green olives
½ cup firmly packed fresh basil leaves
2 teaspoons finely grated lemon rind
8 slices (280g) crusty bread, toasted

1 Heat oil in large saucepan; cook onion, garlic and chilli, stirring, until onion softens. Add wine; bring to the boil. Reduce heat; simmer, uncovered, until liquid is reduced by half.
2 Add undrained tomatoes and the water; bring to the boil. Reduce heat; simmer, uncovered, about 15 minutes or until mixture thickens slightly.
3 Add squid, olives and half the basil; cook about 3 minutes or until squid is tender.
4 Remove from heat; season to taste. Stir in remaining basil and rind. Serve squid with toasted bread.

prep + cook time 30 minutes **serves** 4
nutritional count per serving 14.3g total fat (2.5g saturated fat); 2211kJ (529 cal); 49.3g carbohydrate; 42g protein; 6.1g fibre

Brown rice paella

8 uncooked large king prawns (shrimp) (560g)
500g (1 pound) small black mussels
600g (1¼ pounds) squid hoods, cleaned
1 uncooked blue swimmer crab (325g)
1 tablespoon olive oil
6 green onions (scallions), chopped coarsely
2 cloves garlic, crushed
1 fresh long red chilli, chopped finely
1 medium yellow capsicum (bell pepper) (200g), chopped coarsely
2 cups (400g) brown medium-grain rice
pinch saffron threads
1 cup (250ml) dry white wine
4 medium tomatoes (600g), chopped coarsely
1 tablespoon tomato paste
1 litre (4 cups) chicken stock

1 Shell and devein prawns, leaving tails intact. Scrub mussels; remove beards. Cut squid down centre to open out; score inside in diagonal pattern then cut into thick strips.
2 To prepare crab, lift tail flap then, with a peeling motion, lift off the back shell. Remove and discard whitish gills, liver and brain matter. Rinse crab under cold water; cut crab in quarters.
3 Heat oil in large deep frying pan; cook onion, garlic, chilli and capsicum, stirring, until onion softens. Add rice and saffron; stir to coat in onion mixture. Stir in wine, tomato and paste; cook, stirring, until wine has almost evaporated.
4 Add 1 cup of stock; cook, stirring, until absorbed. Add remaining stock; cook, covered, stirring occasionally, about 1 hour or until rice is tender.
5 Uncover pan; place seafood on top of rice (do not stir to combine). Cover pan; simmer about 5 minutes or until seafood has changed in colour and mussels have opened (discard any that do not). Season to taste.

prep + cook time 1 hour 45 minutes **serves** 4
nutritional count per serving 10g total fat (2.1g saturated fat); 2759kJ (660 cal); 85.4g carbohydrate; 43.2g protein; 5.4g fibre
tip Never wash seafood under a running tap as this will wash away the "sea" flavour and waterlog the seafood. If you need to rinse, hold the seafood in one hand over the sink and use your other hand to gently splash the seafood with as little water as possible.

Mussels with tomato and chilli

1 tablespoon olive oil
4 shallots (100g), sliced thinly
4 cloves garlic, sliced thinly
3 fresh long red chillies, sliced thinly lengthways
1 cup (250ml) dry white wine
800g (1½ pounds) canned cherry tomatoes
2kg (4 pounds) pot-ready black mussels
½ cup coarsely chopped fresh flat-leaf parsley

1 Heat oil in large saucepan; cook shallot, garlic and chilli, stirring, until fragrant.
2 Stir in wine and undrained tomatoes; bring to the boil. Add mussels; cook, covered, about 3 minutes or until mussels open (discard any that do not). Season to taste; stir in parsley.

prep + cook time 25 minutes **serves** 4
nutritional count per serving 6.9g total fat (1.2g saturated fat); 899kJ (215 cal); 12.2g carbohydrate; 14.3g protein; 3.5g fibre
tip Pot-ready mussels have been scrubbed and bearded and are ready to cook.

Paella valenciana

500g (1 pound) clams
1 tablespoon coarse cooking salt
  (kosher salt)
300g (9½ ounces) medium
  uncooked king prawns (shrimp)
500g (1 pound) small black
  mussels
1 pinch saffron threads
¼ cup (60ml) hot water
2 tablespoons olive oil
2 chicken thigh fillets (400g),
  chopped coarsely
1 cured chorizo sausage (170g),
  sliced thinly

1 large red onion (300g),
  chopped finely
1 medium red capsicum (bell
  pepper) (200g), chopped finely
2 cloves garlic, crushed
2 teaspoons sweet paprika
1½ cups (300g) white medium-
  grain rice
3½ cups (875ml) chicken stock
1 cup (120g) frozen peas
2 medium tomatoes (300g),
  peeled, seeded, chopped finely

1 Rinse clams under cold water; place in large bowl, sprinkle with salt, cover with cold water, stand 2 hours. Discard water; rinse clams thoroughly, drain. Shell and devein prawns, leaving tails intact. Scrub mussels, remove beards. Combine saffron and the hot water in small bowl; stand 30 minutes.
2 Heat oil in 40cm (16-inch) wide shallow pan; cook chicken until browned. Remove from pan.
3 Cook chorizo in same pan until browned; drain on absorbent paper. Add onion, capsicum, garlic and paprika; cook stirring, until soft. Add rice; stir to coat in onion mixture. Return chicken and chorizo to pan.
4 Stir in stock and saffron mixture; bring to the boil. Reduce heat; simmer, uncovered, about 12 minutes or until rice is almost tender. Sprinkle peas and tomato over rice; simmer, uncovered, 3 minutes.
5 Place clams, mussels and prawns over rice mixture (do not stir to combine); cover pan. Simmer about 5 minutes or until prawns change colour and clams and mussels have opened (discard any that do not). Season to taste.

prep + cook time 1 hour (+ standing) **serves** 4
nutritional count per serving 31.4g total fat (8.9g saturated fat); 3319kJ (794 cal); 72.4g carbohydrate; 53.2g protein; 4.7g fibre
tips The traditional paella pan is shallow and wide. If you don't have one, use one large or two smaller frying pans – the mixture should only be about 4cm (1½ inches) deep. This recipe is best made just before serving.

Clams with white wine and tomatoes

2.5kg (5 pounds) clams
½ cup (125ml) dry white wine
½ cup (125ml) olive oil
1 small red onion (100g), chopped finely
2 cloves garlic, crushed
2 tablespoons lemon juice
2 tablespoons white wine vinegar
5 large tomatoes (1.1kg), chopped coarsely
4 green onions (scallions), sliced thinly
2 tablespoons coarsely chopped fresh coriander (cilantro)

1 Rinse clams under cold water; place in large bowl of cold salted water, stand 2 hours. Discard water then rinse clams thoroughly; drain.
2 Place clams in large saucepan with wine. Cover; bring to the boil. Reduce heat; simmer about 5 minutes or until clams open (discard any that do not). Drain clams; discard liquid.
3 Heat one tablespoon of the oil in same pan; cook red onion and garlic, stirring, until browned lightly. Add combined juice, vinegar and remaining oil; cook, stirring, about 2 minutes or until thickened slightly.
4 Return clams to pan with tomato, green onion and coriander; toss gently to combine. Season to taste.

prep + cook time 40 minutes (+ standing) **serves** 4
nutritional count per serving 29.3g total fat (4.2g saturated fat); 1802kJ (431 cal); 9.1g carbohydrate; 25.3g protein; 4.1g fibre

Prawn and chorizo skewers with bean and tomato salad

24 uncooked medium king prawns (shrimp) (1kg)
4 cloves garlic, crushed
2 tablespoons olive oil
150g (4½ ounces) green beans, trimmed, halved
3 medium egg (plum) tomatoes (225g), quartered
2 tablespoons roasted pine nuts
¼ cup coarsely chopped fresh flat-leaf parsley
8 x 20cm (8-inch) stalks fresh rosemary
2 cured chorizo sausages (340g), sliced thickly
lime mustard dressing
2 tablespoons olive oil
2 tablespoons lime juice
1 tablespoon wholegrain mustard
2 cloves garlic, crushed

1 Shell and devein prawns, leaving tails intact. Combine prawns in medium bowl with garlic and oil. Cover; refrigerate 3 hours or overnight.
2 Make lime mustard dressing.
3 Meanwhile, boil, steam or microwave beans until tender; drain. Rinse under cold water; drain. Place beans in medium bowl with tomato, nuts, parsley and dressing; toss gently to combine. Season to taste.
4 Drain prawns; discard marinade. Remove leaves from bottom two-thirds of each rosemary stalk; thread prawns and chorizo, alternately, onto rosemary skewers.
5 Cook skewers on heated oiled grill plate (or grill or barbecue) until prawns are changed in colour and chorizo is browned.
6 Serve skewers with bean and tomato salad.
lime mustard dressing Place ingredients in screw-top jar; shake well.

prep + cook time 35 minutes (+ refrigeration) **serves** 4
nutritional count per serving 49.9g total fat (12.3g saturated fat); 2730kJ (653 cal); 5.4g carbohydrate; 45g protein; 3.4g fibre

Seafood soup

1 tablespoon olive oil
3 rindless bacon slices (195g), sliced thinly
1 medium brown onion (150g), chopped finely
1 small fennel bulb (200g), sliced thinly
3 cloves garlic, sliced thinly
2 medium tomatoes (300g), seeded, chopped coarsely
2 tablespoons tomato paste
1 teaspoon hot paprika
½ cup (125ml) dry white wine
800g (1½ pounds) canned whole tomatoes
3 cups (750ml) fish stock
1 litre (4 cups) water
500g (1 pound) kipfler potatoes, cut into 2.5cm (1-inch) pieces
1.2kg (2½ pounds) marinara mix
½ cup coarsely chopped fresh flat-leaf parsley

1 Heat oil in large saucepan; cook bacon, stirring, until crisp. Drain on absorbent paper.
2 Add onion, fennel and garlic to pan; cook, stirring, until vegetables soften. Add fresh tomato; cook, stirring, until soft. Add tomato paste and paprika; cook, stirring, 2 minutes. Return bacon to pan with wine; cook, stirring, 2 minutes.
3 Slice canned tomatoes thickly, then add with juice from can to pan; add stock, the water and potato. Bring to the boil. Reduce heat; simmer, covered, about 20 minutes or until potato is tender.
4 Add marinara mix; cook, covered, about 3 minutes or until seafood is cooked. Season to taste; stir in parsley.

prep + cook time 50 minutes **serves** 6
nutritional count per serving 8.8g total fat (2.2g saturated fat); 1781kJ (426 cal); 24.5g carbohydrate; 50.5g protein; 5.7g fibre
tip We used a marinara mix with mussels in their shells.

Salt cod with roasted tomatoes

1.5kg (3 pounds) salted cod fillets, skin on
6 large tomatoes (1.3kg)
½ cup (125ml) olive oil
1 medium brown onion (150g), chopped coarsely
2 dried ancho chillies
¼ cup (60ml) boiling water
500g (1 pound) baby new potatoes, halved

4 medium brown onions (600g), chopped finely
6 cloves garlic, crushed
1 teaspoon smoked paprika
1 cup (150g) pimiento-stuffed green olives
½ cup coarsely chopped fresh parsley

1 Rinse fish under cold water to remove excess salt. Place fish in large bowl, cover with cold water; refrigerate, covered, overnight, changing the water three or four times. Drain fish; discard water.
2 Preheat oven to 200°C/400°F.
3 Remove cores from tops of tomatoes; cut a small cross in the skin at base of each tomato. Place on oiled oven tray, drizzle with 1 tablespoon of the oil; roast 15 minutes or until tomatoes begin to soften. When cool enough to handle, peel away skins.
4 Meanwhile, place fish in large saucepan with coarsely chopped onion, cover with water; bring to the boil. Reduce heat; simmer, uncovered, 15 minutes or until fish is cooked. Drain fish; discard liquid and onion. Remove skin and bones from fish; flake fish into 4cm (1½-inch) pieces.
5 Place chillies in bowl, cover with the boiling water; stand 10 minutes. Drain; discard liquid. Remove stems, seeds and membranes from chillies; chop chillies. Blend or process tomatoes and chillies until smooth.
6 Boil, steam or microwave potatoes until tender; drain.
7 Heat remaining oil in large frying pan; cook finely chopped onion and garlic, stirring, until onion is softened and browned lightly. Add paprika; cook, stirring, 1 minute. Add tomato mixture, fish, potatoes, olives and parsley; season to taste, stir gently until heated through.

prep + cook time 50 minutes (+ refrigeration & standing) **serves** 6
nutritional count per serving 3.8g total fat (0.6g saturated fat); 589kJ (141 cal); 3.1g carbohydrate; 22.7g protein; 1.2g fibre
tip Salted cod, also called salt cod, baccalà, bacalhau, bacalao and morue, is available from Italian, Spanish and Portuguese delicatessens and some specialty food stores. It needs to be de-salted and rehydrated before use.

Prawn and chorizo sauté with orange

500g (1 pound) uncooked medium king prawns (shrimp)
2 cured chorizo sausages (340g), sliced thinly
1 large red onion (300g), chopped coarsely
2 medium red capsicums (bell peppers) (400g), chopped coarsely
1 teaspoon sweet smoked paprika
2 tablespoons red wine vinegar
1 teaspoon finely grated orange rind
2 teaspoons olive oil
1 medium orange (240g), segmented
1 cup loosely packed fresh flat-leaf parsley leaves

1 Shell and devein prawns, leaving tails intact.
2 Place prawns in large bowl with chorizo, onion, capsicum, paprika, vinegar and rind; toss gently to combine.
3 Heat oil in large frying pan; cook prawn mixture until vegetables are tender and prawns are changed in colour.
4 Remove pan from heat, add orange and parsley, season to taste; toss gently to combine.

prep + cook time 25 minutes **serves** 4
nutritional count per serving 28.5g total fat (9.6g saturated fat); 1852kJ (443 cal); 13g carbohydrate; 32.5g protein; 3.9g fibre

Pan-fried fish with fennel and olive salad

4 x 200g (6½-ounce) white fish fillets, skin-on
2 medium red capsicums (bell peppers) (400g), chopped coarsely
2 small fennel (400g), trimmed, sliced thinly
½ cup (60g) seeded black olives
⅓ cup coarsely chopped fresh basil
2 tablespoons olive oil
1 tablespoon balsamic vinegar

1 Cook fish, skin-side down, in heated oiled large frying pan, turning once, until cooked as desired.
2 Meanwhile, place remaining ingredients in medium bowl, season to taste; toss gently to combine.
3 Serve fish with salad.

prep + cook time 20 minutes **serves** 4
nutritional count per serving 13.9g total fat (2.7g saturated fat); 1409kJ (337 cal); 8.6g carbohydrate; 42.9g protein; 2.8g fibre
tip We used blue-eye in this recipe but you can use any white fish fillets you like.

Roasted fish with tomatoes, capsicums and olives

1 medium red onion (170g), cut into thick wedges
2 medium red capsicums (bell peppers) (400g), sliced thickly
250g (8 ounces) cherry tomatoes
4 cloves garlic, unpeeled, bruised
2 tablespoons extra virgin olive oil
1kg (2-pound) whole snapper, cleaned
1 cup (120g) seeded green olives
¼ cup coarsely chopped fresh flat-leaf parsley
1 medium lemon (140g), cut into wedges

1 Preheat oven to 220°C/425°F.
2 Combine onion, capsicum, tomatoes, garlic and half the oil in large baking dish; roast, uncovered, 20 minutes.
3 Pat fish dry, inside and out, with absorbent paper. Score fish three times on both sides. Place fish on top of vegetables in dish, drizzle with remaining oil.
4 Roast, uncovered, about 20 minutes or until fish is cooked through.
5 Transfer fish to platter; cover to keep warm. Stir olives and parsley into vegetable mixture; season to taste.
6 Serve fish with vegetable mixture and lemon wedges.

prep + cook time 55 minutes **serves** 4
nutritional count per serving 11.3g total fat (1.9g saturated fat); 1058kJ (253 cal); 14.1g carbohydrate; 22g protein; 3.6g fibre
tip We used snapper in this recipe but you can use any whole white fish you like.

Fish with green sauce and white bean puree

1 tablespoon olive oil
1 clove garlic, crushed
1 medium brown onion (150g), chopped finely
1.2kg (2½ pounds) canned white beans, rinsed, drained
1 cup (250ml) chicken stock
¼ cup (60ml) pouring cream
4 x 200g (6½-ounce) white fish fillets, skin-on
green sauce
½ cup finely chopped fresh flat-leaf parsley
¼ cup each finely chopped fresh mint, dill and chives
1 tablespoon wholegrain mustard
2 tablespoons lemon juice
2 tablespoons rinsed, drained baby capers, chopped finely
1 clove garlic, crushed
¼ cup (60ml) olive oil

1 Make green sauce.
2 Heat oil in medium saucepan; cook garlic and onion, stirring, until onion softens. Add beans and stock; bring to the boil. Reduce heat; simmer, uncovered, until liquid has almost evaporated. Stir in cream; blend or process bean mixture until smooth. Season to taste.
3 Meanwhile, cook fish, skin-side down, in heated oiled large frying pan, turning once, until cooked as desired.
4 Serve fish on white bean puree, topped with green sauce.
green sauce Combine ingredients in small bowl.

prep + cook time 55 minutes **serves** 4
nutritional count per serving 23.5g total fat (4.4g saturated fat); 1789kJ (428 cal); 7.4g carbohydrate; 46.9g protein; 5.6g fibre
tips Many varieties of already cooked white beans are available canned, among them cannellini (which is what we used), butter and haricot beans; any of these are suitable for this recipe.
We used kingfish in this recipe but you can use any white fish fillets you like.

179

Fish parcels with anchovies and olives

4 x 200g (6½-ounce) white fish fillets
2 teaspoons fresh rosemary leaves
4 drained anchovy fillets, chopped finely
2 teaspoons finely grated lemon rind
2 cloves garlic, sliced thinly
½ cup (60g) seeded black olives
¼ cup coarsely chopped fresh flat-leaf parsley
1 tablespoon olive oil

1 Preheat oven to 220°C/425°F.
2 Divide fish among four 30cm (12-inch) squares of baking paper. Top fish with combined remaining ingredients; season. Fold paper over fish, tucking ends under to secure.
3 Place parcels on oven tray; bake about 12 minutes or until fish is cooked through.

prep + cook time 25 minutes **serves** 4
nutritional count per serving 9.4g total fat (2.1g saturated fat); 1124kJ (269 cal); 3.6g carbohydrate; 42.1g protein; 0.7g fibre
serving suggestion Radicchio, rocket and tomato salad.

Barbecued salmon with capsicum and olive salsa

cooking-oil spray
1.5kg (3 pound) side of salmon, skin-on
2 teaspoons coarse cooking salt (kosher salt)
½ cup loosely packed fresh small basil leaves
capsicum and olive salsa
1 large red capsicum (bell pepper) (350g)
125g (4 ounces) cherry tomatoes, halved
2 tablespoons rinsed, drained baby capers
¼ cup (60g) seeded green olives, quartered
¼ cup (60ml) olive oil

1 Make capsicum and olive salsa.
2 Place double layer of foil about 1 metre (39 inches) long on bench; spray with cooking oil. Place a 45cm (17½-inch) sheet of baking paper in centre of foil.
3 Pat salmon dry with absorbent paper; rub salt over skin. Place salmon, skin-side-down, onto baking paper. Fold foil and baking paper to enclose salmon securely.
4 Cook salmon parcel, skin-side-down, on heated oiled grill plate (or grill or barbecue), over medium heat, about 10 minutes or until cooked to your liking.
5 Just before serving, stir basil into salsa; serve salmon topped with salsa.
capsicum and olive salsa Preheat grill (broiler). Quarter capsicum; discard seeds and membranes. Cook capsicum, skin-side-up, under grill until skin blisters and blackens. Cover capsicum with paper or plastic; stand 5 minutes. Peel away skins; cut into 2cm (¾-inch) pieces. Place capsicum in medium bowl with tomato, capers, olives and oil; toss gently to combine.

prep + cook time 40 minutes **serves** 8
nutritional count per serving 20.3g total fat (4g saturated fat); 1455kJ (348 cal); 3.8g carbohydrate; 37.3g protein; 0.9g fibre
tip The salmon can be prepared and wrapped up to one hour ahead. The salsa can be made two hours ahead; add basil just before serving.

Char-grilled octopus and artichoke salad

1 cup loosely packed fresh dill
1kg (2 pounds) cleaned baby octopus, halved
¼ cup (60ml) mustard seed oil
2 teaspoons finely grated lemon rind
¼ cup (60ml) lemon juice
500g (1 pound) marinated artichokes, drained

1 Coarsely chop half the dill; combine in large bowl with octopus, oil, rind and juice.
2 Cook octopus mixture on heated oiled grill plate (or grill or barbecue) about 2 minutes or until tender.
3 Combine octopus with artichokes and remaining dill in large bowl; season to taste.

prep + cook time 35 minutes **serves** 4
nutritional count per serving 18.6g total fat (2.7g saturated fat); 1881kJ (450 cal); 4g carbohydrate; 65.3g protein; 2.5g fibre

Fish with spiced chickpeas

4 cleaned whole small white fish (800g)
1 tablespoon lemon juice
1 teaspoon each sweet paprika and ground cumin
1 clove garlic, crushed
2 tablespoons olive oil
1 teaspoon cumin seeds
1 teaspoon ground coriander
½ teaspoon ground turmeric
800g (1½ pounds) canned chickpeas (garbanzo beans), rinsed, drained
⅓ cup (80ml) chicken stock
1 fresh small red thai (serrano) chilli, chopped finely
3 medium tomatoes (450g), chopped coarsely
⅓ cup coarsely chopped fresh coriander (cilantro)

1 Pat fish dry, inside and out, with absorbent paper. Combine juice, paprika, ground cumin, garlic and half the oil in large bowl; add fish, turn to coat in spice mixture.
2 Cook fish on heated oiled grill plate (or grill or barbecue) until browned both sides and cooked through.
3 Meanwhile, dry-fry seeds and spices in medium saucepan until fragrant. Add remaining oil and chickpeas to pan, then stock and chilli; cook, stirring, until hot. Remove from heat; stir in tomato and coriander. Season to taste.
4 Serve fish with chickpeas.

prep + cook time 30 minutes **serves** 4
nutritional count per serving 14.4g total fat (2.5g saturated fat); 1480kJ (354 cal); 20.7g carbohydrate; 31.5g protein; 7.8g fibre
tip We used whiting in this recipe.
serving suggestion Low-fat natural yogurt and lemon wedges.

Lemon and herb fish with chickpea salad

2 tablespoons olive oil
½ teaspoon dried chilli flakes
1 cup finely shredded fresh basil
4 x 200g (6½-ounce) white fish fillets, skin-on
2 cloves garlic, sliced thinly
800g (1½ pounds) canned chickpeas (garbanzo beans), rinsed, drained
½ cup (125ml) chicken stock
270g (8½ ounces) bottled roasted red capsicum (bell pepper) in oil,
    drained, sliced thickly
1 medium lemon (140g)

1 Combine half the oil with chilli and a third of the basil in medium bowl. Cut two slits in skin of each fish fillet; add fish to oil mixture, turn to coat in mixture.
2 Cook fish, skin-side down, in heated oiled large frying pan 2 minutes; turn, cook a further 3 minutes or until cooked through. Transfer to plate; cover, stand 5 minutes.
3 Heat remaining oil in same pan; cook garlic, stirring, 30 seconds. Add chickpeas, stock and capsicum; simmer, uncovered, about 3 minutes or until stock is almost evaporated.
4 Meanwhile, using a vegetable peeler, peel rind from lemon; slice rind thinly. Juice lemon; add 2 tablespoons of juice to chickpeas with rind. Season to taste; stir in remaining basil.
5 Serve fish with chickpea salad.

prep + cook time 25 minutes **serves** 4
nutritional count per serving 19.6g total fat (3.4g saturated fat); 1965kJ (470 cal); 19.5g carbohydrate; 50.3g protein; 7.2g fibre

Scallop and fish skewers
with tomato salad

500g (1 pound) white fish fillets, cut into 2cm (¾-inch) pieces
500g (1 pound) scallops, roe removed
⅓ cup finely chopped fresh basil
¼ cup (60ml) red wine vinegar
2 tablespoons olive oil
3 large egg (plum) tomatoes (270g), cut into 1cm (½-inch) pieces
250g (8 ounces) yellow teardrop tomatoes, halved
250g (8 ounces) cherry tomatoes, halved
½ cup loosely packed fresh basil leaves, torn
red wine vinaigrette
2 tablespoons red wine vinegar
¼ cup (60ml) olive oil
1 teaspoon dijon mustard
1 teaspoon white (granulated) sugar

1 Thread fish and scallops, alternately, onto 12 bamboo skewers; place in large shallow dish, drizzle with combined chopped basil, vinegar and oil.
2 Make red wine vinaigrette.
3 Cook skewers on heated oiled grill plate (or grill or barbecue) until cooked as desired.
4 Meanwhile, combine tomatoes, torn basil and vinaigrette in medium bowl; season to taste.
5 Serve skewers with salad.
red wine vinaigrette Place ingredients in screw-top jar; shake well.

prep + cook time 40 minutes **serves** 4
nutritional count per serving 26.6g total fat (4.3g saturated fat);
1831kJ (438 cal); 6g carbohydrate; 41.5g protein; 3.1g fibre
tips Soak skewers in cold water before use to prevent them from splintering or scorching during cooking.
We used blue-eye in this recipe but you can use any white fish you like.

Garlic prawn, capsicum and artichoke salad

1kg (2 pounds) uncooked large king prawns (shrimp)
4 cloves garlic, crushed
1 fresh small red thai (serrano) chilli, chopped finely
2 tablespoons olive oil
500g (1 pound) small jerusalem artichokes
1 medium red capsicum (bell pepper) (200g)
100g (3 ounces) baby rocket leaves (arugula)
caper dressing
¼ cup (60ml) lemon juice
2 tablespoons olive oil
1 tablespoon rinsed, drained capers, chopped finely
1 teaspoon dijon mustard

1 Shell and devein prawns, leaving tails intact. Combine prawns, garlic, chilli and half the oil in large bowl.
2 Make caper dressing.
3 Scrub artichokes under cold water; halve lengthways. Toss artichokes with remaining oil in medium bowl; cook on heated oiled grill plate (or grill or barbecue) until tender.
4 Meanwhile, quarter capsicums; discard seeds and membranes. Cook capsicum on heated oiled grill plate (or grill or barbecue) until tender; slice thickly.
5 Cook prawns on same grill plate (or grill or barbecue) until changed in colour.
6 Place prawns, artichokes and capsicum in large bowl with rocket and dressing; toss gently to combine.
caper dressing Place ingredients in screw-top jar; shake well.

prep + cook time 30 minutes **serves** 4
nutritional count per serving 19.5g total fat (2.7g saturated fat); 1371kJ (328 cal); 13.8g carbohydrate; 29.4g protein; 4.5g fibre

Crisp-skinned fish with paprika mustard butter

¼ cup (60ml) olive oil
6 x 200g (6½-ounce) white fish fillets, skin-on
1 small red onion (100g), chopped finely
2 cured chorizo sausages (340g), chopped coarsely
250g (8 ounces) cherry tomatoes, halved
400g (12½ ounces) canned cannellini beans, rinsed, drained
200g (6½ ounces) baby spinach leaves
paprika mustard butter
125g (4 ounces) butter, softened
2 teaspoons each dijon and wholegrain mustard
½ teaspoon ground paprika
1 tablespoon finely grated lemon rind
1 tablespoon finely chopped fresh flat-leaf parsley

1 Preheat oven to 200°C/400°F.
2 Make paprika mustard butter.
3 Heat 2 tablespoons of the oil in large frying pan; cook fish, skin-side down, in batches, about 5 minutes or until skin is crisp. Transfer fish, skin-side up, to foil-lined oven tray; roast, in oven, about 6 minutes or until fish is cooked to your liking. Remove from oven, cover loosely with foil; stand 5 minutes.
4 Meanwhile, heat remaining oil in same cleaned pan; cook onion, stirring, until softened. Add chorizo; cook, stirring, 1 minute. Stir in tomato and beans. Reduce heat; cook about 2 minutes or until beans are heated through. Stir in spinach; season to taste.
5 Divide bean mixture among serving plates, top with fish and a slice of paprika mustard butter.

paprika mustard butter Beat butter in small bowl with electric mixer until soft. Beat in remaining ingredients; season. Form mixture into log, roll in plastic wrap; refrigerate or freeze until firm.

prep + cook time 40 minutes (+ refrigeration) **serves** 6
nutritional count per serving 47.9g total fat (20.2g saturated fat); 2792kJ (668 cal); 4.8g carbohydrate; 54.3g protein; 3.1g fibre
tip We used blue-eye fillets in this recipe.

Fish stew with saffron, tomato and wine

500g (1 pound) uncooked medium king prawns (shrimp)
500g (1 pound) small black mussels
1 tablespoon olive oil
1 medium brown onion (150g), chopped finely
3 cloves garlic, crushed
1 small leek (200g), sliced thinly
1 small fennel bulb (200g), sliced thinly
1 stalk celery (150g), trimmed, sliced thinly
½ cup (125ml) dry white wine
800g (1½ pounds) canned diced tomatoes
1 litre (4 cups) fish stock
pinch saffron threads
200g (6½ ounces) kipfler potatoes, cut into 1cm (½-inch) slices
300g (9½ ounces) white fish fillet, chopped coarsely
300g (9½ ounces) salmon fillet, chopped coarsely

1 Shell and devein prawns. Scrub mussels; remove beards.
2 Heat oil in large saucepan; cook onion, garlic, leek, fennel and celery, stirring, about 10 minutes or until vegetables soften.
3 Add wine, undrained tomatoes, stock, saffron and potato to pan; bring to the boil. Reduce heat; simmer, uncovered, about 10 minutes or until potato is tender.
4 Add prawns and fish to pan; cook, uncovered, 5 minutes. Add mussels; cook, covered, about 2 minutes or until mussels open (discard any that do not). Season to taste.

prep + cook time 50 minutes **serves** 6
nutritional count per serving 9g total fat (1.9g saturated fat);
1254kJ (300 cal); 13.5g carbohydrate; 35.4g protein; 4.3g fibre
tip As a general rule, we do not recommend freezing cooked seafood of any kind because it tends to undergo both textural and flavour changes.

Barbecued seafood with aïoli

500g (1 pound) uncooked medium king prawns (shrimp)
½ cup (125ml) olive oil
1 clove garlic, crushed
1 teaspoon sweet paprika
2 teaspoons finely grated lemon rind
650g (1¼ pounds) white fish fillets
2 large zucchini (300g), sliced thickly lengthways
1 large red capsicum (bell pepper) (350g), quartered
1 medium lemon (140g), cut into wedges
aïoli
½ cup (150g) mayonnaise
1 clove garlic, crushed
1 tablespoon lemon juice

1 Make aïoli.
2 Shell and devein prawns, leaving tails intact. Place prawns in large bowl with oil, garlic, paprika, rind and fish; toss to combine, season.
3 Cook vegetables on heated oiled grill plate (or grill or barbecue) until tender. Remove from heat; cover to keep warm.
4 Cook seafood on same heated grill plate (or grill or barbecue) until prawns are changed in colour and fish is cooked through.
5 Serve seafood and vegetables with aïoli and lemon wedges.
aïoli Combine ingredients in small bowl.

prep + cook time 35 minutes **serves** 4
nutritional count per serving 45g total fat (6.6g saturated fat);
2721kJ (651 cal); 12.3g carbohydrate; 48.6g protein; 3g fibre
tip We used whiting fillets in this recipe but you can use any white fish fillets you like.

Poultry

Spicy chicken, capsicum and tomato rice

2 teaspoons olive oil
1 large brown onion (200g), chopped coarsely
2 cloves garlic, crushed
2 medium green capsicums (bell peppers) (400g), chopped coarsely
16 chicken drumettes (2kg)
410g (13 ounces) canned tomato puree
1 teaspoon hot paprika
1 tablespoon each ground coriander and ground cumin
½ teaspoon cayenne pepper
2 cups (320g) fresh corn kernels
½ cup (125ml) dry red wine
1 cup (250ml) chicken stock
2 dried bay leaves
1½ cups (300g) white long-grain rice
2 tablespoons finely chopped fresh flat-leaf parsley

1 Preheat oven to 200°C/400°F.
2 Heat oil in large flameproof casserole dish; cook onion, garlic and capsicum, stirring, until vegetables soften. Remove vegetables, leaving as much oil in dish as possible.
3 Cook chicken in same dish, in batches, until browned. Remove from dish.
4 Return chicken and vegetables to dish with tomato puree, spices, corn, wine, stock, bay leaves and rice; bring to the boil. Cover; cook in oven about 30 minutes or until rice is tender and chicken is cooked through. Season to taste. Serve sprinkled with parsley.

prep + cook time 1 hour **serves** 8
nutritional count per serving 17.1g total fat (4.8g saturated fat); 1919kJ (459 cal); 41.5g carbohydrate; 30.2g protein; 3.9g fibre
tip Chicken drumettes are drumsticks with the end of the bone chopped off. They are also sold as "lovely legs".
serving suggestion Steamed green beans and crunchy bread rolls.

Chicken and potato casserole with pine nuts

1 tablespoon olive oil
4 chicken drumsticks (600g)
4 chicken thigh cutlets (800g)
1 large brown onion (200g), chopped finely
4 medium potatoes (800g), quartered
½ cup (80g) pine nuts, roasted
½ cup (80g) blanched almonds, roasted
3 cups (750ml) chicken stock
1 cup (250ml) dry white wine
⅓ cup (80ml) lemon juice
4 cloves garlic, crushed
2 tablespoons fresh thyme leaves
½ cup coarsely chopped fresh flat-leaf parsley
500g (1 pound) baby green beans, trimmed

1 Preheat oven to 180°C/350°F.
2 Heat oil in large flameproof casserole dish; cook chicken, in batches, until browned. Remove from dish.
3 Cook onion in same dish, stirring, until softened. Return chicken to dish with potato, nuts, stock, wine, juice, garlic, thyme and half the parsley; bring to the boil. Cover; cook in oven about 1 hour or until chicken is cooked through. Season to taste.
4 Meanwhile, boil, steam or microwave beans until tender; drain.
5 Sprinkle chicken with remaining parsley; serve with beans.

prep + cook time 1 hour 35 minutes **serves** 4
nutritional count per serving 61.4g total fat (12.4g saturated fat); 4050kJ (969 cal); 35g carbohydrate; 57g protein; 10.4g fibre
tip When using wine in cooking, as a general rule of thumb you should never cook with a wine you wouldn't drink; the wine you use doesn't have to be expensive, but it does have to be drinkable. If you don't want to use white wine, you could substitute water, ginger ale or white grape juice.

Chorizo-stuffed roast chicken

20g (¾ ounce) butter
1 medium brown onion (150g), chopped finely
1 cured chorizo sausage (170g), cut into 1cm (½-inch) pieces
1½ cups (110g) stale breadcrumbs
½ cup (100g) ricotta cheese
1 egg, beaten lightly
¼ cup finely chopped fresh flat-leaf parsley
¼ cup (35g) slivered almonds, roasted
1.6kg (3¼-pound) chicken
2 medium lemons (280g), cut into wedges
spinach and red onion salad
150g (4½ ounces) baby spinach leaves
1 small red onion (100g), sliced thinly
1 tablespoon red wine vinegar
2 tablespoons olive oil

1 Melt half the butter in medium frying pan; cook onion and chorizo, stirring, until onion softens. Cool 10 minutes; combine chorizo mixture in medium bowl with breadcrumbs, cheese, egg, parsley and nuts, season.
2 Preheat oven to 200°C/400°F.
3 Wash chicken under cold water; pat dry inside and out with absorbent paper. Tuck wing tips under chicken. Trim skin around neck; secure neck flap to underside of chicken with skewers.
4 Fill cavity with chorizo mixture, fold over skin to enclose stuffing; secure with toothpicks. Tie legs together with kitchen string. Place chicken and lemon in medium baking dish. Rub chicken all over with remaining butter, season; roast, uncovered, about 1½ hours or until chicken is cooked through, basting occasionally with juices.
5 Meanwhile, make spinach and red onion salad.
6 Serve chicken with stuffing, lemon and salad.
spinach and red onion salad Combine ingredients in large bowl.

prep + cook time 2 hours **serves** 4
nutritional count per serving 68.4g total fat (21.4g saturated fat); 4042kJ (967 cal); 24.4g carbohydrate; 60.3g protein; 5.8g fibre

Chicken with almond sauce

¼ cup (60ml) olive oil
½ cup (125ml) orange juice
3 cloves garlic, crushed
6 x 200g (6½-ounce) chicken breast fillets
3 small fennel bulbs (600g)
2 medium red onions (340g)
1 tablespoon olive oil, extra
almond sauce
1 tablespoon olive oil
¼ cup (15g) stale breadcrumbs
¾ cup (90g) ground almonds
pinch ground cloves
1 cup (250ml) chicken stock
2 tablespoons dry white wine
¼ cup (60ml) thickened (heavy) cream

1 Combine oil, juice, garlic and chicken in medium bowl. Cook chicken on heated oiled grill plate (or grill or barbecue) until browned and cooked through. Remove from heat; cover to keep warm.
2 Meanwhile, cut fennel and onions into wedges. Heat extra oil in large frying pan; cook fennel and onion, stirring, until onions are soft and browned lightly. Remove from heat; cover to keep warm.
3 Make almond sauce.
4 Serve chicken with fennel mixture and sauce.
almond sauce Heat oil in medium frying pan; cook breadcrumbs, stirring, until browned lightly. Add ground almonds and clove; cook, stirring, until browned lightly. Gradually add combined stock and wine, stir over heat until mixture is smooth; bring to the boil. Remove from heat; stir in cream. Season to taste.

prep + cook time 35 minutes **serves** 6
nutritional count per serving 35.8g total fat (7.8g saturated fat); 2174kJ (520 cal); 9.5g carbohydrate; 37.7g protein; 4.1g fibre

209

Chicken with chocolate sauce

6 x 500g (1-pound) small chickens
⅓ cup (50g) plain (all-purpose) flour
¼ cup (60ml) olive oil
1 medium brown onion (150g), chopped finely
2 cloves garlic, crushed
1 cinnamon stick
¼ teaspoon ground cloves
½ teaspoon ground nutmeg
800g (1½ pounds) canned crushed tomatoes
1 large red capsicum (bell pepper) (350g), sliced thinly
1 cup (250ml) dry white wine
60g (2 ounces) dark eating (semi-sweet) chocolate, chopped finely
⅓ cup coarsely chopped fresh flat-leaf parsley

1 Rinse chickens under cold water; pat dry with absorbent paper.
Using kitchen scissors, cut along sides of chickens' backbones;
discard backbones. Halve chickens along breastbones then cut each
half into two pieces.
2 Coat chicken in flour; shake off excess. Heat oil in large frying pan;
cook chicken, in batches, until browned. Drain on absorbent paper.
3 Cook onion and garlic in same pan, stirring, until onion softens.
Add spices, cook, stirring, until fragrant.
4 Return chicken to pan with undrained tomatoes, capsicum and wine;
simmer, covered, 20 minutes. Uncover; simmer about 20 minutes or
until chicken is tender and sauce thickens slightly. Add chocolate;
cook, stirring, until smooth. Discard cinnamon stick; season to taste.
Serve chicken with sauce; sprinkle with parsley.

prep + cook time 1 hour 20 minutes **serves** 6
nutritional count per serving 51.9g total fat (15.3g saturated fat);
3294kJ (788 cal); 20.1g carbohydrate; 52.8g protein; 3.3g fibre
serving suggestion Crusty bread to mop up the juices, steamed green
beans and rice or a green salad.

Braised chicken with chickpeas, lemon and garlic

1 tablespoon olive oil
2 medium brown onions (300g), sliced thickly
2 teaspoons smoked paprika
3 cloves garlic, crushed
8 chicken thigh cutlets, skin removed (1.6kg)
3 cups (750ml) salt-reduced chicken stock
¼ cup (60ml) lemon juice
2 fresh long red chillies, halved lengthways
800g (1½ pounds) canned chickpeas (garbanzo beans), rinsed, drained
2 teaspoons dijon mustard
½ cup coarsely chopped fresh flat-leaf parsley
2 teaspoons finely grated lemon rind

1 Heat oil in large saucepan; cook onion, stirring, until softened. Add paprika, garlic and chicken; stir to coat chicken in onion mixture.
2 Add stock, juice, chilli, chickpeas and mustard to pan; bring to the boil. Reduce heat; simmer, covered, 30 minutes. Uncover; simmer further 30 minutes or until chicken is tender. Season to taste.
3 Serve chicken sprinkled with parsley and rind.

prep + cook time 1 hour 15 minutes **serves** 4
nutritional count per serving 22.4g total fat (5.6g saturated fat); 2378kJ (569 cal); 24.7g carbohydrate; 63.5g protein; 8.4g fibre

Quail and mushroom paella

4 quails (640g)
2 x 200g (6½-ounce) chicken
  breast fillets
2 fresh small red thai (serrano)
  chillies, chopped finely
2 cloves garlic, crushed
2 tablespoons lemon juice
¼ cup (60ml) olive oil
1 medium brown onion (150g),
  sliced thinly
250g (8 ounces) button
  mushrooms, sliced thinly
100g (3 ounces) swiss brown
  mushrooms, sliced thinly

1 small red capsicum (bell pepper)
  (150g), sliced thinly
1 small green capsicum (bell
  pepper) (150g), sliced thinly
2 cups (400g) white long-grain rice
1.25 litres (5 cups) chicken stock
pinch saffron threads
¾ cup (90g) frozen peas, thawed
2 medium tomatoes (300g),
  peeled, seeded, chopped finely
2 tablespoons finely chopped
  fresh flat-leaf parsley

1 Rinse quails under cold water; pat dry with absorbent paper. Discard necks from quails. Using kitchen scissors, cut along sides of quails' backbones; discard backbones. Halve quails along breastbones. Cut each chicken breast into three pieces.

2 Combine quail, chicken, chilli, garlic and juice in large bowl. Cover; refrigerate 3 hours or overnight.

3 Heat oil in 40cm (16-inch) wide shallow pan; cook quail and chicken, in batches, until browned. Remove from pan; cover to keep warm.

4 Drain all but 2 tablespoons of oil from pan. Cook onion, mushrooms and capsicum in same pan, stirring, until vegetables soften. Stir in rice, stock and saffron; bring to the boil. Reduce heat; simmer, uncovered, about 10 minutes or until most of the liquid is absorbed.

5 Place chicken and quail over rice mixture; sprinkle with peas and tomato (do not stir to combine). Simmer, uncovered, about 5 minutes or until rice is tender. Season to taste. Serve sprinkled with parsley.

prep + cook time 45 minutes (+ refrigeration) **serves** 4
nutritional count per serving 32.9g total fat (7.5g saturated fat); 3658kJ (875 cal); 89.4g carbohydrate; 51.9g protein; 6.2g fibre
tips The traditional paella pan is shallow and wide. If you don't have one, use one large or two smaller frying pans – the mixture should only be about 4cm (1½ inches) deep. This recipe is best made just before serving.

Grilled chicken with green olive butter

400g (12½ ounces) baby new potatoes, sliced thickly
800g (1½ pounds) chicken breast fillets
150g (4½ ounces) baby spinach leaves
green olive butter
100g (3 ounces) butter, softened
¾ cup (90g) seeded green olives, chopped coarsely
1 teaspoon finely grated lemon rind
1 clove garlic, crushed
1 tablespoon coarsely chopped fresh basil

1 Make green olive butter.
2 Boil, steam or microwave potato until tender; drain. Cover to keep warm.
3 Meanwhile, halve chicken fillets horizontally. Cook chicken on heated oiled grill plate (or grill or barbecue).
4 Divide potato among plates; top with spinach, chicken then olive butter.
green olive butter Combine ingredients in small bowl.

prep + cook time 35 minutes **serves** 4
nutritional count per serving 32g total fat (17g saturated fat); 2316kJ (554 cal); 18.6g carbohydrate; 46.5g protein; 3.5g fibre

Chicken, capsicum and bean stew

1 tablespoon vegetable oil
8 chicken drumsticks (1.2kg)
1 large red onion (300g), sliced thickly
2 cloves garlic, crushed
2 fresh long red chillies, chopped finely
1 teaspoon ground cumin
4 medium tomatoes (600g), chopped coarsely
1 cup (250ml) chicken stock
⅓ cup loosely packed fresh oregano leaves
400g (12½ ounces) canned kidney beans, rinsed, drained
1 medium yellow capsicum (bell pepper) (200g), sliced thickly
1 medium green capsicum (bell pepper) (200g), sliced thickly

1 Heat half the oil in large saucepan; cook chicken, in batches, until browned. Remove from pan.
2 Heat remaining oil in pan; cook onion, garlic, chilli and cumin, stirring, until onion softens. Return chicken to pan with tomato, stock and ¼ cup of the oregano; bring to the boil. Reduce heat; simmer, covered, 30 minutes.
3 Add beans and capsicum to pan; simmer, uncovered, 20 minutes. Season to taste.
4 Divide stew among serving bowls; sprinkle with remaining oregano.

prep + cook time 1 hour 20 minutes **serves** 4
nutritional count per serving 26.5g total fat (7.1g saturated fat); 2090kJ (500 cal); 19g carbohydrate; 42.6g protein; 8.4g fibre
serving suggestion Sour cream.

Grilled paprika and chilli chicken with spanish rice

⅓ cup (80ml) lemon juice
1 tablespoon olive oil
1 tablespoon sweet paprika
2 teaspoons dried oregano
2 fresh small red thai (serrano) chillies, chopped finely
1 clove garlic, crushed
4 x 200g (6½-ounce) chicken thigh fillets, halved
⅓ cup (110g) tomato chutney or salsa
spanish rice
1 tablespoon olive oil
4 green onions (scallions), chopped finely
1 clove garlic, crushed
1 medium red capsicum (bell pepper) (200g), chopped finely
125g (4 ounces) canned corn kernels, rinsed, drained
3 cups (450g) cooked white long-grain rice
⅓ cup (40g) seedless green olives, chopped coarsely
¼ cup finely chopped fresh coriander (cilantro)

1 Combine juice, oil, paprika, oregano, chilli, garlic and chicken in large bowl; season. Cook chicken mixture on heated oiled grill plate (or grill or barbecue), covered loosely with foil, until browned both sides and cooked through.
2 Meanwhile, make spanish rice.
3 Serve chicken with spanish rice and tomato chutney or salsa.
spanish rice Heat oil in large frying pan; cook onion, garlic, capsicum and corn, stirring, until vegetables soften. Add rice; cook, stirring, about 5 minutes or until heated through. Stir in olives and coriander; season to taste.

prep + cook time 35 minutes **serves** 4
nutritional count per serving 24.3g total fat (5.8g saturated fat); 2521kJ (603 cal); 51.4g carbohydrate; 42.8g protein; 2.7g fibre
tips For a more intense flavour, marinate the chicken overnight. You will need to cook 1 cup (200g) white long-grain rice for the amount of cooked rice needed for this recipe.

Chicken and chorizo salad with garlic mayonnaise

1 cured chorizo sausage (170g), sliced thinly
600g (1¼ pounds) chicken breast fillets
¾ cup (110g) pimiento-stuffed green olives
3 pieces bottled roasted red capsicum (bell pepper) (125g),
    drained, sliced thinly
½ small red onion (50g), sliced thinly
2 cups loosely packed fresh flat-leaf parsley leaves
⅓ cup (55g) almond kernels, roasted
1 medium lemon (140g), cut into wedges
garlic mayonnaise
½ cup (150g) whole-egg mayonnaise
1 clove garlic, crushed
½ teaspoon smoked paprika
1 tablespoon lemon juice

1 Make garlic mayonnaise.
2 Cook chorizo in heated medium frying pan until browned and crisp;
drain on absorbent paper.
3 Cook chicken in same pan until browned and cooked through.
Remove from pan; cover, stand 5 minutes then slice thinly.
4 Meanwhile, combine olives, capsicum, onion, parsley, nuts and
chorizo in large bowl; season to taste.
5 Divide salad among serving plates; top with sliced chicken and
garlic mayonnaise. Serve with lemon wedges.
garlic mayonnaise Combine ingredients in small bowl.

prep + cook time 40 minutes **serves** 4
nutritional count per serving 43g total fat (9.4g saturated fat);
2604kJ (623 cal); 11.6g carbohydrate; 45g protein; 5.9g fibre
tip The garlic mayonnaise can be thinned with a little boiling water,
if you prefer.

Chicken in almond pomegranate sauce

2 medium pomegranates (640g)
1½ cups (375ml) water
⅓ cup (75g) firmly packed light brown sugar
2 tablespoons olive oil
4 x 200g (6½-ounce) chicken breast fillets
1 large brown onion (200g), sliced thickly
2 cloves garlic, crushed
1 tablespoon plain (all-purpose) flour
1 teaspoon each sweet paprika, ground cumin and ground coriander
½ teaspoon ground cinnamon
½ cup (125ml) chicken stock
⅓ cup (55g) blanched almonds, roasted
⅓ cup coarsely chopped fresh coriander (cilantro)

1 Cut pomegranates in half, scoop out pulp. Reserve about ⅓ cup pulp. Place remaining pulp in small saucepan with the water and sugar; stir over heat, without boiling, until sugar dissolves. Simmer, uncovered, 5 minutes; strain syrup into medium heatproof jug.
2 Heat half the oil in large frying pan; cook chicken, in batches, until browned. Remove from pan.
3 Heat remaining oil in same pan; cook onion and garlic, stirring, until onion softens. Add flour and spices; cook, stirring, about 1 minute or until mixture is just browned and dry. Gradually stir in stock and pomegranate syrup; cook, stirring, until mixture boils and thickens slightly.
4 Return chicken to pan; simmer, covered, about 5 minutes or until cooked through. Stir in reserved pomegranate pulp, nuts and coriander; season to taste.

prep + cook time 35 minutes **serves** 4
nutritional count per serving 28g total fat (5.3g saturated fat); 2366kJ (566 cal); 29.3g carbohydrate; 47.8g protein; 4.8g fibre
tip Pomegranate pulp consists of the seeds and the edible pulp surrounding them; it has a tangy sweet-sour flavour.

225

Coriander and chilli grilled chicken

6 chicken thigh fillets (1.2kg), halved
coriander chilli sauce
8 green onions (scallions), chopped coarsely
3 cloves garlic, quartered
3 fresh small red thai (serrano) chillies, chopped coarsely
¼ cup loosely packed fresh coriander leaves
1 teaspoon white (granulated) sugar
¼ cup (60ml) lime juice
chickpea salad
600g (1¼ pounds) canned chickpeas, rinsed, drained
2 medium egg (plum) tomatoes (150g), chopped coarsely
2 green onions (scallions), chopped finely
2 tablespoons lime juice
1 cup coarsely chopped fresh coriander (cilantro)
1 tablespoon olive oil

1 Make coriander chilli sauce.
2 Cook chicken on heated oiled grill plate (or grill or barbecue) until almost cooked through. Brush about two-thirds of the coriander chilli sauce all over chicken; cook further 5 minutes or until chicken is cooked through.
3 Make chickpea salad.
4 Sprinkle chicken with remaining coriander chilli sauce; serve with chickpea salad.
coriander chilli sauce Blend or process onion, garlic, chilli, coriander and sugar until finely chopped. Add juice; blend until well combined. Season to taste.
chickpea salad Combine ingredients in large bowl.

prep + cook time 25 minutes **serves** 4
nutritional count per serving 18.5g total fat (4.6g saturated fat); 1651kJ (395 cal); 15.9g carbohydrate; 38.3g protein; 6.2g fibre

Chicken in red wine and tomato sauce

30g (1 ounce) butter
2 tablespoons olive oil
2 medium white onions (300g), sliced thinly
2 cloves garlic, crushed
750g (1½ pounds) chicken thigh fillets, halved
250g (8 ounces) button mushrooms, sliced thinly
800g (1½ pounds) canned crushed tomatoes
¼ cup (70g) tomato paste
¼ cup (60ml) dry red wine
2 teaspoons light brown sugar
1 teaspoon cracked black peppercorns
½ cup (125ml) chicken stock
¼ cup coarsely chopped fresh basil

1 Heat butter and oil in large frying pan; cook onion and garlic, stirring, until onion softens. Add chicken; cook, stirring, until browned and almost cooked through.
2 Stir in mushrooms, undrained tomatoes, paste, wine, sugar, peppercorns and stock; bring to the boil. Reduce heat; simmer, uncovered, until chicken is cooked and sauce thickens slightly. Remove from heat; season to taste, stir in basil.

prep + cook time 30 minutes **serves** 4
nutritional count per serving 29.7g total fat (9.5g saturated fat); 2128kJ (509 cal); 14.8g carbohydrate; 41g protein; 6.1g fibre

Chicken with lentil salsa

12 chicken tenderloins (900g)
2 teaspoons each ground cumin and ground coriander
1 teaspoon ground turmeric
1½ cups (300g) red lentils
1 clove garlic, crushed
1 fresh small red thai (serrano) chilli, chopped finely
1 lebanese cucumber (130g), seeded, chopped finely
1 medium red capsicum (bell pepper) (200g), chopped finely
¼ cup (60ml) lemon juice
2 teaspoons peanut oil
2 tablespoons coarsely chopped fresh coriander (cilantro)
2 limes, cut into wedges

1 Combine chicken and spices in medium bowl.
2 Cook lentils in large saucepan of boiling water, uncovered, until tender; drain. Rinse under cold water; drain.
3 Place lentils in large bowl with garlic, chilli, cucumber, capsicum, juice, oil and fresh coriander; toss gently to combine. Season to taste.
4 Cook chicken on heated oiled grill plate (or grill or barbecue) until cooked through. Cook limes on same grill plate until browned both sides.
5 Serve chicken with lentil salsa and lime wedges.

prep + cook time 25 minutes **serves** 4
nutritional count per serving 9.1g total fat (2g saturated fat);
2157kJ (516 cal); 31.6g carbohydrate; 70.2g protein; 11.7g fibre

Quail, fig and orange salad

6 quails (1.2kg)
3 medium oranges (720g)
4 medium fresh figs (240g), quartered
100g (3 ounces) mizuna
½ cup (60g) coarsely chopped roasted pecans
honey orange dressing
⅓ cup (80ml) orange juice
¼ cup (60ml) olive oil
2 tablespoons honey
1 clove garlic, crushed

1 Make honey orange dressing.
2 Rinse quails under cold water; pat dry with absorbent paper. Discard necks from quails. Using kitchen scissors, cut along sides of quails' backbones; discard backbones. Halve quails along breastbones; brush quail with half the dressing. Cook quail on heated oiled grill plate (or grill or barbecue), uncovered, until cooked through.
3 Meanwhile, segment oranges over large bowl; add remaining ingredients and remaining dressing, toss gently to combine.
4 Divide salad among serving plates; top with quails.
honey orange dressing Place ingredients in screw-top jar; shake well. Season to taste.

prep + cook time 35 minutes **serves** 4
nutritional count per serving 41.4g total fat (7g saturated fat); 2604kJ (623 cal); 29.3g carbohydrate; 32g protein; 6g fibre
tip Mizuna, originating from Japan, are frizzy green salad leaves with a delicate mustard flavour.

Chicken sofrito

4 chicken breast fillets (800g)
2 tablespoons lime juice
¼ cup (60ml) chilli sauce
2 cloves garlic, crushed
20g (¾ ounce) butter
2 medium brown onions (300g), sliced thickly
2 tablespoons red wine vinegar
¼ cup (55g) white (granulated) sugar
1 tablespoon chilli sauce, extra
¼ cup (60ml) water
¼ cup (60ml) orange juice
6 medium egg (plum) tomatoes (450g), cut into wedges
1 tablespoon drained bottled jalapeño chillies, chopped coarsely
3 green onions (scallions), sliced thickly

1 Combine chicken, juice, sauce and garlic in large bowl.
2 Heat butter in large saucepan; cook brown onion, stirring, until softened. Add vinegar and sugar; cook, stirring, 2 minutes. Stir in extra sauce, the water and juice; add tomato and chilli, stir until heated through. Season to taste.
3 Meanwhile, cook drained chicken, on heated oiled grill plate (or grill or barbecue) until browned and cooked through. Slice thickly.
4 Serve chicken with sofrito; sprinkle with green onion.

prep + cook time 30 minutes **serves** 4
nutritional count per serving 15.9g total fat (6.2g saturated fat);
1827kJ (437 cal); 25.7g carbohydrate; 45.6g protein; 3.7g fibre

Lemon thyme and chilli roast chicken

5 small chickens (2.5kg)
1 tablespoon fresh lemon thyme leaves
lemon thyme and chilli marinade
2 fresh long red chillies, chopped finely
2 cloves garlic, crushed
1 tablespoon fresh lemon thyme leaves
2 teaspoons finely grated lemon rind
¼ cup (60ml) lemon juice
2 tablespoons olive oil
2 tablespoons sherry vinegar
2 tablespoons honey

1 Make lemon thyme and chilli marinade.
2 Rinse chickens under cold water; pat dry with absorbent paper.
Using kitchen scissors, cut along side of chickens' backbones; discard
backbones. Halve chickens along breastbones then cut each half into
two pieces.
3 Combine three-quarters of the marinade with chicken in large shallow
dish. Cover; refrigerate 3 hours or overnight. Refrigerate remaining
marinade until required.
4 Preheat oven to 220°C/425°F.
5 Place chicken, in single layer, on wire racks in large shallow baking
dishes. Roast about 40 minutes or until cooked.
6 Serve chicken drizzled with reserved marinade and sprinkled with
thyme leaves.
lemon thyme and chilli marinade Place ingredients in screw-top jar;
shake well. Season to taste.

prep + cook time 1 hour 10 minutes (+ refrigeration) **serves** 10
nutritional count per serving 23.4g total fat (6.7g saturated fat);
1367kJ (327 cal); 5g carbohydrate; 24.6g protein; 0.1g fibre
serving suggestion Green salad, steamed green beans, grilled
flatbread and lemon wedges.

Quail with tomatoes and mint dressing

6 quails (1.2kg)
1 teaspoon ground cumin
3 cloves garlic, crushed
¼ cup (60ml) olive oil
2 medium tomatoes (300g), seeded, chopped finely
mint dressing
½ cup (125ml) olive oil
⅓ cup (80ml) white wine vinegar
1 tablespoon finely shredded fresh mint

1 Preheat oven to 180°C/350°F.
2 Rinse quails under cold water; pat dry with absorbent paper. Discard necks from quails. Using kitchen scissors, cut along sides of quails' backbones; discard backbones. Halve quails along breastbones. Combine quail, cumin, garlic and 1 tablespoon of the oil in large bowl.
3 Heat remaining oil in large frying pan; cook quail, in batches, until browned. Remove from pan.
4 Place quail, skin-side up, in single layer on oven tray; cook, in oven, about 15 minutes or until cooked through.
5 Meanwhile, make mint dressing.
6 Serve quail drizzled with dressing; sprinkle with tomato.
mint dressing Place ingredients in screw-top jar; shake well. Season to taste.

prep + cook time 40 minutes (+ refrigeration) **serves** 6
nutritional count per serving 39.1g total fat (6.9g saturated fat); 1789kJ (428 cal); 0.6g carbohydrate; 18.9g protein; 0.5g fibre
tip For a more intense flavour, combine cooked quail and mint dressing in large bowl; cover, refrigerate 3 hours or overnight. Remove from refrigerator about 30 minutes before serving. Stir in tomato.

Chicken, fennel, olive and orange salad

30g (1 ounce) butter
3 chicken breast fillets (600g), sliced thinly
1 large fennel bulb (550g), sliced thinly
½ cup (60g) seeded black olives, quartered
3 green onions (scallions), chopped coarsely
2 medium oranges (480g), segmented
80g (2½ ounces) baby rocket leaves (arugula)
orange dressing
½ cup (125ml) orange juice
2 tablespoons red wine vinegar
2 tablespoons olive oil
½ teaspoon white (granulated) sugar

1 Melt butter in large frying pan; cook chicken, stirring, until browned and cooked through.
2 Meanwhile, make orange dressing.
3 Place chicken in large bowl with fennel, olives, onion, orange segments, rocket and dressing; toss gently to combine. Season to taste.
orange dressing Place ingredients in screw-top jar; shake well.

prep + cook time 25 minutes **serves** 4
nutritional count per serving 19.2g total fat (6.3g saturated fat); 1647kJ (394 cal); 16.4g carbohydrate; 36.6g protein; 4.6g fibre

Meat

Pork ribs with chorizo and smoked paprika

1.5kg (3 pounds) american-style pork spareribs
4 cloves garlic, crushed
2 teaspoons smoked paprika
1 tablespoon olive oil
1 cured chorizo sausage (170g), sliced thinly
1 tablespoon olive oil, extra
1 medium red onion (170g), chopped coarsely
1 medium red capsicum (bell pepper) (200g), chopped coarsely
1 tablespoon light brown sugar
800g (1½ pounds) canned chopped tomatoes
1 cup (250ml) chicken stock

1 Cut between bones of pork to separate into individual ribs.
Combine garlic, paprika and olive oil in small bowl; rub over pork ribs.
2 Preheat oven to 160°C/325°F.
3 Cook chorizo in heated large flameproof baking dish, stirring, until browned lightly. Remove from dish with slotted spoon; drain on absorbent paper.
4 Cook ribs, in same dish, in batches, until browned. Drain on absorbent paper.
5 Add extra oil, onion and capsicum to same dish; cook, stirring, until onion softens. Return ribs and chorizo to dish with sugar, undrained tomatoes and stock; bring to the boil.
6 Cover dish tightly with foil; cook, in oven, 1 hour. Remove foil; cook further 30 minutes or until ribs are tender. Season to taste.

prep + cook time 2 hours 15 minutes **serves** 4
nutritional count per serving 38.5g total fat (11.4g saturated fat); 2516kJ (602 cal); 15.6g carbohydrate; 49.2g protein; 4.1g fibre

Barbecued leg of lamb with chorizo

2.5kg (5-pound) leg of lamb
2 cured chorizo sausages (340g), chopped coarsely
10 cloves garlic, halved
1 tablespoon sweet paprika
1 tablespoon olive oil
½ cup (125ml) dry sherry

1 Place lamb in large baking dish, make deep slits all over with sharp knife; push chorizo and garlic into slits.
2 Combine paprika, oil and sherry in small bowl, season; rub paprika mixture all over lamb. Cover; refrigerate 3 hours or overnight, turning lamb occasionally.
3 Drain lamb; discard marinade. Cook lamb, covered, on heated barbecue, using indirect heat, about 1 hour 40 minutes or until cooked as desired. Cover lamb; stand 20 minutes before serving.

prep + cook time 1 hour 50 minutes (+ refrigeration) **serves** 10
nutritional count per serving 19.5g total fat (8.4g saturated fat); 1547kJ (370 cal); 1g carbohydrate; 45.1g protein; 0.8g fibre
tip Lamb can also be roasted, uncovered, in oven preheated to 200°C/400°F for about 1½ hours or until cooked as desired.

Shredded beef soup

500g (1-pound) piece beef skirt steak
2 litres (8 cups) water
1 dried bay leaf
6 black peppercorns
1 large carrot (180g), chopped coarsely
1 stalk celery (150g), trimmed, chopped coarsely
1 tablespoon olive oil
1 medium brown onion (150g), sliced thickly
1 medium red capsicum (bell pepper) (200g), sliced thickly
1 medium green capsicum (bell pepper) (200g), sliced thickly
2 cloves garlic, crushed
2 fresh long red chillies, chopped finely
1 teaspoon ground cumin
400g (12½ ounces) canned crushed tomatoes
⅓ cup loosely packed fresh oregano leaves
1 trimmed corn cob (250g)

1 Tie beef with kitchen string at 2.5cm (1-inch) intervals. Place in large saucepan with the water, bay leaf, peppercorns, carrot and celery; bring to the boil. Reduce heat; simmer, covered, 1½ hours. Uncover; simmer about 30 minutes or until beef is tender. Cool beef in stock 10 minutes.
2 Transfer beef to large bowl; using two forks, shred beef coarsely. Strain stock through muslin-lined sieve over another large heatproof bowl; discard solids.
3 Heat oil in same cleaned pan; cook onion, capsicum, garlic, chilli and cumin, stirring, until vegetables soften. Return beef and stock to pan with undrained tomatoes and ¼ cup of the oregano; bring to the boil. Reduce heat; simmer, uncovered, 10 minutes.
4 Cut corn kernels from cob. Add corn to soup; cook, uncovered, until just tender. Season to taste.
5 Serve soup sprinkled with remaining oregano.

prep + cook time 2 hours 40 minutes **serves** 4
nutritional count per serving 9g total fat (2g saturated fat); 1413kJ (338 cal); 25.9g carbohydrate; 34.3g protein; 7.4g fibre
serving suggestion Toasted flour tortillas.

Seared calves liver
with caramelised onion

5 small red onions (500g), sliced thinly
1 tablespoon light brown sugar
1½ tablespoons sherry vinegar
3 medium potatoes (600g), unpeeled, cut into 1cm (½-inch) slices
1 tablespoon olive oil
600g (1¼ pounds) calves liver, sliced thinly

1 Cook onion in heated oiled large frying pan, stirring occasionally,
until browned lightly. Add sugar and vinegar; cook, stirring, until onion
is caramelised. Transfer onion to small bowl; cover to keep warm.
2 Meanwhile, boil, steam or microwave potato until tender; drain,
combine in large bowl with oil. Cook potato on heated oiled grill plate
(or grill or barbecue) until browned. Transfer potato to medium bowl;
cover to keep warm.
3 Cook liver on same grill plate (or grill or barbecue) until browned both
sides and just cooked. Serve liver with onion and potatoes.

prep + cook time 45 minutes **serves** 4
nutritional count per serving 13.1g total fat (3.3g saturated fat);
1660kJ (397 cal); 34.2g carbohydrate; 33g protein; 4g fibre
tip Calves liver should be cut into paper-thin slices then quickly seared
because too much cooking will destroy its soft, delicate texture. Your
butcher will slice the liver thinly for you.

Spanish shredded beef

2 litres (8 cups) water
1 dried bay leaf
5 cloves garlic, quartered
6 black peppercorns
1 large carrot (180g), chopped coarsely
1 stalk celery (150g), trimmed, chopped coarsely
1.5kg (3 pounds) beef skirt steak
2 teaspoons dried oregano
1 tablespoon olive oil
1 medium red capsicum (bell pepper) (200g), sliced thickly
1 medium green capsicum (bell pepper) (200g), sliced thickly
2 medium brown onions (300g), sliced thickly

400g (12½ ounces) canned whole tomatoes
1 teaspoon ground cumin
1 cup (150g) pimiento-stuffed green olives, halved
¼ cup (60ml) lemon juice

sofrito
1 tablespoon olive oil
2 rindless bacon slices (130g), chopped finely
3 cloves garlic, crushed
1 small brown onion (80g), chopped finely
½ small green capsicum (bell pepper) (75g), chopped finely
1 tablespoon tomato paste
2 tablespoons red wine vinegar

1 Combine the water, bay leaf, garlic, peppercorns, carrot, celery, beef and 1 teaspoon of the oregano in large saucepan; bring to the boil. Reduce heat; simmer, uncovered, about 2 hours or until beef is tender.
2 Meanwhile, make sofrito.
3 Transfer beef to large bowl; using two forks, shred beef coarsely. Strain braising liquid through muslin-lined sieve over another large heatproof bowl; discard solids.
4 Heat oil in same cleaned pan; cook sofrito, capsicums and onion, stirring, until vegetables soften. Return beef and braising liquid to pan with undrained tomatoes, cumin and remaining oregano; bring to the boil. Reduce heat; simmer, uncovered, 20 minutes. Remove from heat; stir in olives and juice. Season to taste.
sofrito Heat oil in small frying pan; cook bacon, garlic, onion and capsicum, stirring, until onion softens. Add paste and vinegar; cook, stirring, until vinegar evaporates. Cool 10 minutes; blend or process until smooth.

prep + cook time 3 hours **serves** 6
nutritional count per serving 17.5g total fat (4.7g saturated fat); 1969kJ (471 cal); 11g carbohydrate; 64g protein; 6.2g fibre
serving suggestion Serve with rice and peas.

Pork belly and chorizo stew

2 cured chorizo sausages (340g), sliced thinly
600g (1¼-pound) piece pork belly, rind removed,
    cut into 2.5cm (1-inch) pieces
1 large brown onion (200g), sliced thinly
2 cloves garlic, crushed
1 teaspoon sweet smoked paprika
1 large red capsicum (bell pepper) (350g), chopped coarsely
800g (1½ pounds) canned chopped tomatoes
½ cup (125ml) dry red wine
½ cup (125ml) water
400g (12½ ounces) canned white beans, rinsed, drained
½ cup finely chopped fresh flat-leaf parsley

1 Cook chorizo and pork, in batches, in heated large flameproof casserole dish, stirring, until browned. Remove from dish.
2 Add onion and garlic to dish; cook, stirring, until onion softens. Return meats to dish with paprika, capsicum, undrained tomatoes, wine and the water; bring to the boil. Reduce heat; simmer, covered, 40 minutes.
3 Add beans; simmer, uncovered, about 20 minutes or until pork is tender and sauce thickens slightly. Season to taste.
4 Serve stew sprinkled with parsley.

prep + cook time 1 hour 35 minutes **serves** 4
nutritional count per serving 55g total fat (19.1g saturated fat); 3331kJ (797 cal); 26.7g carbohydrate; 47g protein; 7.9g fibre
tip Many varieties of already cooked white beans are available canned, among them cannellini (which is what we used), butter and haricot beans; any of these are suitable for this stew.

Rabbit stew

2 tablespoons oil
1kg (2 pounds) rabbit pieces
3 medium brown onions (450g), sliced thickly
4 cloves garlic, crushed
1 cup (250ml) water
1 litre (4 cups) chicken stock
400g (12½ ounces) canned diced tomatoes
5 medium potatoes (1kg), chopped coarsely
2 medium carrots (240g), sliced thickly
1 tablespoon balsamic vinegar
3 dried bay leaves
1 teaspoon dried chilli flakes
⅓ cup coarsely chopped fresh mint
1 cup (120g) frozen peas

1 Heat half the oil in large saucepan; cook rabbit, in batches, until browned. Remove from pan.
2 Heat remaining oil in same pan; cook onion and garlic, stirring, until onion softens.
3 Return rabbit to pan with the water, stock, undrained tomatoes, potato, carrot, vinegar, bay leaves, chilli and mint; bring to the boil. Reduce heat; simmer, uncovered, 1¼ hours. Add peas; simmer, uncovered, 5 minutes. Season to taste.

prep + cook time 2 hours **serves** 4
nutritional count per serving 19.4g total fat (5.1g saturated fat); 2750kJ (658 cal); 44.4g carbohydrate; 70.7g protein; 10.6g fibre

Smoky sausages and beans

1 cup (200g) dried kidney beans
800g (1½ pounds) beef sausages, chopped coarsely
1 tablespoon olive oil
1 large white onion (200g), chopped coarsely
3 cloves garlic, crushed
1 large red capsicum (bell pepper) (350g), chopped coarsely
½ teaspoon ground cumin
2 teaspoons sweet smoked paprika
1 teaspoon dried chilli flakes
800g (1½ pounds) canned crushed tomatoes
2 tablespoons coarsely chopped fresh oregano

1 Place beans in medium bowl, cover with cold water; stand overnight, drain. Rinse under cold water; drain. Add beans to medium saucepan of boiling water; return to the boil. Reduce heat; simmer, uncovered, about 30 minutes or until beans are almost tender. Drain.
2 Cook sausages, in batches, in large saucepan until browned. Drain on absorbent paper.
3 Heat oil in same pan; cook onion, garlic and capsicum, stirring, until onion softens. Add spices and chilli; cook, stirring, about 2 minutes or until fragrant. Add beans and undrained tomatoes; bring to the boil. Reduce heat; simmer, covered, about 1 hour or until beans are tender.
4 Return sausages to pan; simmer, covered, about 10 minutes or until sausages are cooked through. Remove from heat; season to taste, stir in oregano.

prep + cook time 2 hours 30 minutes (+ standing) **serves** 4
nutritional count per serving 56.9g total fat (25.2g saturated fat); 3323kJ (795 cal); 33.5g carbohydrate; 38.1g protein; 20.2g fibre
serving suggestion Flour tortillas.

Braised lamb shanks

1 tablespoon olive oil
8 french-trimmed lamb shanks (2kg)
1 large red onion (300g), chopped coarsely
2 cloves garlic, crushed
1 cup (250ml) chicken stock
2 cups (500ml) water
400g (12½ ounces) canned diced tomatoes
1 tablespoon fresh rosemary leaves
4 drained anchovy fillets, chopped coarsely
2 large red capsicums (bell peppers) (700g)
2 large green capsicums (bell peppers) (700g)

1 Heat oil in large saucepan; cook lamb, in batches, until browned.
Remove from pan.
2 Cook onion and garlic in same pan, stirring, until onion softens. Add
stock, the water, undrained tomatoes, rosemary and anchovy; bring to the
boil. Return lamb to pan, reduce heat; simmer, covered, 1 hour, stirring
occasionally. Uncover; simmer about 45 minutes or until lamb is tender.
3 Meanwhile, quarter capsicums; discard seeds and membranes. Roast
under hot grill (broiler) or in very hot oven, skin-side up, until skin blisters
and blackens. Cover capsicum pieces with plastic wrap or paper for
5 minutes; peel away skin, slice thickly.
4 Add capsicum to lamb; cook, uncovered, 5 minutes. Season to taste.

prep + cook time 3 hours **serves** 4
nutritional count per serving 30.2g total fat (12.1g saturated fat);
2533kJ (606 cal); 17g carbohydrate; 63.9g protein; 5.4g fibre
serving suggestion Mashed potato, white bean puree or steamed rice.

Chorizo and potato tortilla

800g (1½ pounds) russet burbank potatoes, sliced thinly
1 tablespoon olive oil
1 large brown onion (200g), sliced thinly
200g (6½ ounces) cured chorizo sausage, sliced thinly
6 eggs, beaten lightly
1¼ cups (310ml) pouring cream
4 green onions (scallions), sliced thickly
¼ cup (25g) coarsely grated mozzarella cheese
¼ cup (30g) coarsely grated cheddar cheese

1 Boil, steam or microwave potato until tender; drain.
2 Meanwhile, heat oil in medium frying pan; cook brown onion, stirring, until softened. Add chorizo; cook, stirring, until crisp. Drain chorizo mixture on absorbent paper.
3 Whisk eggs in large bowl with cream, green onion and cheeses, season; stir in potato and chorizo mixture.
4 Pour mixture into heated oiled medium frying pan; cook, covered, over low heat, about 10 minutes or until tortilla is just set. Carefully invert tortilla onto plate, then slide back into pan; cook, uncovered, about 5 minutes or until cooked through.

prep + cook time 45 minutes **serves** 4
nutritional count per serving 68.1g total fat (34.1g saturated fat); 3683kJ (881 cal); 32.6g carbohydrate; 32.7g protein; 4.1g fibre
tips You can also use bintje or pink fir apple potatoes for this recipe. It is fine to use just one 300ml carton of cream for this recipe.

Lentil and chorizo sofrito

1 tablespoon olive oil
4 cured chorizo sausages (680g), sliced thinly
1 medium brown onion (150g), chopped finely
6 rindless bacon slices (390g), sliced thinly
2 cloves garlic, sliced thinly
2½ cups (500g) brown lentils
2 medium carrots (240g), chopped finely
1kg (2 pounds) baby new potatoes, halved
2 dried bay leaves
1.5 litres (6 cups) water
4 medium zucchini (480g), sliced thickly
¼ cup finely chopped fresh flat-leaf parsley
sofrito
4 medium egg (plum) tomatoes (300g), peeled
1 tablespoon olive oil
1 large red onion (300g), sliced thinly

1 Heat oil in large saucepan; cook chorizo, in batches, until browned.
Drain on absorbent paper.
2 Cook onion, bacon and garlic in same pan, stirring, until onion softens.
Return chorizo to pan with lentils, carrot, potato, bay leaves and the water;
bring to the boil. Reduce heat; simmer, covered, about 40 minutes,
stirring occasionally, until lentils are tender and mixture is thick.
3 Meanwhile, make sofrito.
4 Add zucchini to lentil mixture; simmer, covered, about 10 minutes or
until zucchini is tender. Season to taste. Serve lentil mixture topped with
sofrito and parsley.
sofrito Cut tomato into thin wedges. Heat oil in large frying pan; cook
onion, stirring, about 20 minutes or until onion is browned lightly and
softened. Add tomato; cook, stirring gently, until tomato begins to soften.

prep + cook time 1 hour 20 minutes **serves** 8
nutritional count per serving 36g total fat (11.7g saturated fat);
3039kJ (727 cal); 48.8g carbohydrate; 46.7g protein; 14.5g fibre

Chorizo and manchego rolls

3 cured chorizo sausages (510g), sliced thickly
1 cup (280g) mayonnaise
½ teaspoon smoked paprika
8 large bread rolls (600g)
5 hard-boiled eggs, sliced thinly
80g (2½ ounces) baby spinach leaves
150g (4½ ounces) manchego cheese, shaved

1 Cook chorizo in heated oiled large frying pan, in batches, until browned. Drain on absorbent paper.
2 Combine mayonnaise and paprika in small bowl.
3 Split rolls in half; spread mayonnaise mixture over half the roll halves. Top with chorizo, egg, spinach, cheese and remaining roll halves.

prep + cook time 20 minutes **makes** 8
nutritional count per serving 39.9g total fat (12.6g saturated fat); 3018kJ (722 cal); 60.2g carbohydrate; 28.9g protein; 4.1g fibre
tip Manchego cheese is a sharp, firm spanish cheese; it can be found in most specialty food stores and delicatessens. You can use parmesan cheese instead, if manchego is not available. Use a vegetable peeler to shave the cheese.

Winter soup with oxtail and chickpeas

2 tablespoons olive oil
1kg (2 pounds) oxtails, chopped coarsely
4 medium carrots (480g), chopped finely
1 small leek (200g), sliced thinly
4 cloves garlic, sliced thinly
2 stalks celery (300g), trimmed, chopped finely
¼ cup (70g) tomato paste
3 dried bay leaves
2 litres (8 cups) beef stock
1 cured chorizo sausage (170g), chopped finely
400g (12½ ounces) canned chickpeas (garbanzo beans),
    rinsed, drained
½ cup (110g) risoni pasta

1 Heat oil in large saucepan; cook oxtail, in batches, stirring until browned. Remove from pan.
2 Cook carrot, leek, garlic and celery in same pan, stirring, until leek softens. Return oxtail to pan with paste, bay leaves and stock; bring to the boil. Reduce heat; simmer, uncovered, about 3 hours or until meat is tender. Strain soup into large heatproof bowl. Remove meat from oxtail, shred coarsely; discard bones. Return meat and vegetable mixture to soup in bowl; cool. Cover; refrigerate overnight.
3 Remove fat from surface of soup, return soup to cleaned pan; bring to the boil.
4 Meanwhile, cook chorizo in small heated frying pan, stirring, until crisp. Drain on absorbent paper.
5 Add chickpeas and pasta to soup; simmer, covered, about 8 minutes or until pasta is tender. Season to taste. Serve soup topped with chorizo.

prep + cook time 3 hours 30 minutes (+ refrigeration) **serves** 6
nutritional count per serving 36.7g total fat (12.2g saturated fat); 2370kJ (567 cal); 27.8g carbohydrate; 29.1g protein; 6.7g fibre
tip Oxtail is a very fatty cut of meat; this soup must be made a day ahead and refrigerated overnight to remove the excess fat which will solidify on the soup surface after refrigeration. This can simply be scraped off using a large spoon or ladle.

Baked chorizo and white beans

4 cured chorizo sausages (680g), sliced thickly
2 cloves garlic, sliced thinly
2 baby fennel (260g), trimmed, chopped coarsely
400g (12½ ounces) canned chopped tomatoes
⅓ cup (80ml) chicken stock
800g (1½ pounds) canned white beans, rinsed, drained
1 cup (250ml) water
250g (8 ounces) trimmed silver beet (swiss chard), chopped coarsely

1 Preheat oven to 200°C/400°F.
2 Cook chorizo in heated large flameproof dish, stirring, about 5 minutes.
Add garlic and fennel; cook, stirring, 2 minutes.
3 Add undrained tomatoes, stock, beans and the water; cook, in oven,
uncovered, 15 minutes. Stir in silver beet; cook, uncovered, about 5 minutes
or until silver beet wilts. Season to taste.

prep + cook time 35 minutes **serves** 4
nutritional count per serving 52g total fat (18.6g saturated fat);
3214kJ (769 cal); 24.8g carbohydrate; 44.2g protein; 14g fibre
tips You need about 1kg (2 pounds) of untrimmed silver beet to get
the amount needed for this recipe.
Many varieties of already cooked white beans are available canned,
among them cannellini, butter and haricot beans; any of these are
suitable for this recipe.

Slow-roasted spiced lamb shoulder

2 teaspoons fennel seeds
1 teaspoon each ground cinnamon, ginger and cumin
¼ teaspoon chilli powder
2 tablespoons olive oil
1.2kg (2½-pound) lamb shoulder, shank intact
2 cloves garlic, sliced thinly
6 baby brown onions (150g)
375g (12 ounces) baby carrots, trimmed
1 cup (250ml) water

1 Preheat oven to 180°C/350°F.
2 Dry-fry spices in small frying pan until fragrant. Combine spices and half the oil in small bowl.
3 Using sharp knife, score lamb at 2.5cm (1-inch) intervals; push garlic into cuts. Rub lamb all over with spice mixture; season.
4 Heat remaining oil in large flameproof dish; cook lamb, turning, until browned all over. Remove lamb from dish.
5 Meanwhile, peel onions, leaving root ends intact. Add onions to dish; cook, stirring, until browned.
6 Add carrots and the water to dish, bring to the boil; top with lamb, cover loosely with foil. Transfer to oven; roast 1½ hours.
7 Reduce oven to 160°C/325°F.
8 Uncover lamb; roast a further 1½ hours or until lamb is tender. Cover lamb; stand 10 minutes, then slice thinly. Strain pan juices into small heatproof jug.
9 Serve lamb with onions, carrots and pan juices.

prep + cook time 3 hours 30 minutes **serves** 4
nutritional count per serving 21.9g total fat (7.3g saturated fat); 1722kJ (412 cal); 6.5g carbohydrate; 45.7g protein; 3.1g fibre
serving suggestion Steamed green beans.

Spinach, chorizo and roast capsicum salad

2 cured chorizo sausages (340g), sliced thinly
125g (4 ounces) baby spinach leaves
310g (10 ounces) canned chickpeas (garbanzo beans), rinsed, drained
125g (4 ounces) char-grilled red capsicum (bell pepper), sliced thinly
1 tablespoon red wine vinegar

1 Cook chorizo in heated large frying pan until browned both sides. Drain on absorbent paper.
2 Add spinach to same pan; cook, uncovered, until spinach is wilted.
3 Place chorizo and spinach in large bowl with chickpeas, capsicum and vinegar in large bowl; toss gently to combine. Season to taste.

prep + cook time 10 minutes **serves** 4
nutritional count per serving 27.6g total fat (9.6g saturated fat); 1597kJ (382 cal); 11g carbohydrate; 21.1g protein; 4.1g fibre
tip Char-grilled capsicum is available, in slices, from delicatessens, or bottled, in oil or brine, from many supermarkets.

Lamb and chorizo rissoles

750g (1½ pounds) minced (ground) lamb
2 cured chorizo sausages (340g), chopped coarsely
1 small red onion (100g), chopped finely
¼ cup finely chopped fresh flat-leaf parsley
2 teaspoons finely grated lemon rind
2 teaspoons smoked paprika
2 tablespoons olive oil
roast capsicum and caper salad
3 medium red capsicums (bell peppers) (600g)
1 tablespoon olive oil
1 small red onion (100g), sliced thinly
1 cup loosely packed fresh flat-leaf parsley leaves
1 tablespoon drained, rinsed baby capers
1 tablespoon red wine vinegar

1 Combine lamb, chorizo, onion, parsley, rind and paprika in large bowl.
Shape mixture into eight rissoles, place on tray, cover; refrigerate 1 hour.
2 Meanwhile, make roast capsicum and caper salad.
3 Heat oil in large frying pan; cook rissoles, in two batches, about
10 minutes or until browned both sides and cooked through. Drain on
absorbent paper.
4 Serve rissoles with roast capsicum and caper salad.
roast capsicum and caper salad Preheat oven to 200°C/400°F.
Place capsicums on oven tray, drizzle with oil; roast about 30 minutes,
turning occasionally, or until skins blacken. Place capsicums in bowl,
cover, cool. Peel capsicums, discard stems and seeds. Thinly slice
capsicum. Place capsicum in medium bowl with remaining ingredients;
toss gently to combine. Season to taste.

prep + cook time 1 hour 15 minutes (+ refrigeration) **serves** 4
nutritional count per serving 57.7g total fat (19.8g saturated fat);
3252kJ (778 cal); 7.9g carbohydrate; 56.9g protein; 2.7g fibre
tips If you haven't got the time to roast the capsicums, use already
roasted or char-grilled capsicums available from supermarkets and
delicatessens.
Uncooked rissoles can be frozen for up to three months; thaw overnight
in the fridge before cooking.

Veal cutlets with green olive salsa

2 tablespoons olive oil
2 cloves garlic, crushed
1 tablespoon finely chopped fresh oregano
2 teaspoons finely grated lemon rind
1 tablespoon lemon juice
4 x 125g (4-ounce) veal cutlets
green olive salsa
1 tablespoon lemon juice
¼ cup coarsely chopped fresh flat-leaf parsley
½ cup (80g) finely chopped large green olives
1 small green capsicum (bell pepper) (150g), chopped finely
1 tablespoon olive oil
1 clove garlic, crushed
1 tablespoon finely chopped fresh oregano

1 Make green olive salsa.
2 Combine oil, garlic, oregano, rind and juice in small bowl; brush mixture over veal. Cook veal on heated oiled grill plate (or grill or barbecue) until browned both sides and cooked as desired.
3 Serve veal with salsa.
green olive salsa Combine ingredients in small bowl.

prep + cook time 35 minutes **serves** 4
nutritional count per serving 16.3g total fat (2.7g saturated fat); 1112kJ (266 cal); 5.8g carbohydrate; 23.4g protein; 1.2g fibre
serving suggestion Barbecued kipfler potatoes.
To make barbecued kipflers, boil, steam or microwave 1.5kg (3 pounds) kipfler potatoes until tender; drain. Halve potatoes lengthways. Combine ¼ cup fresh thyme leaves, 1 tablespoon coarsely grated lemon rind, 2 crushed garlic cloves, ⅓ cup olive oil, ¼ cup lemon juice and potato in large bowl. Cook potato on heated oiled grill plate (or grill or barbecue) about 15 minutes or until browned.

Green chilli stew

2 tablespoons olive oil
1kg (2 pounds) beef chuck steak, cut into 2.5cm (1-inch) cubes
1 large brown onion (200g), sliced thinly
2 cloves garlic, sliced thinly
2 teaspoons ground cumin
2 long green chillies, sliced thinly
2 cups (500ml) beef stock
1 tablespoon tomato paste
3 large egg (plum) tomatoes (270g), chopped coarsely
500g (1 pound) baby new potatoes, halved
4 small flour tortillas
¼ cup coarsely chopped fresh coriander

1 Heat half the oil in large flameproof baking dish; cook beef, in batches, stirring, until browned all over.
2 Preheat oven to 180°C/350°F.
3 Heat remaining oil in same dish; cook onion, garlic, cumin and chilli, stirring, until onion softens. Add stock and paste; bring to the boil, stirring. Return beef to dish, cover; cook, in oven, 45 minutes.
4 Add tomato and potato; cook, covered, 35 minutes. Uncover; cook 20 minutes. Season to taste.
5 Meanwhile, cut each tortilla into six wedges. Place, in single layer, on oven trays; toast, uncovered, in oven about 8 minutes or until crisp.
6 Stir coriander into stew just before serving with tortilla crisps.

prep + cook time 1 hour 45 minutes **serves** 4
nutritional count per serving 23.4g total fat (6.6g saturated fat); 2604kJ (623 cal); 40.1g carbohydrate; 59.8g protein; 5.6g fibre
tips Round steak, skirt steak and gravy beef are also suitable for this recipe. Tortilla crisps can be prepared up to two days ahead and kept in an airtight container at room temperature.
serving suggestion Grilled cobs of corn.

Chorizo, roasted capsicum and artichoke salad

2 large red capsicums (bell peppers) (700g)
2 cured chorizo sausages (340g), sliced thinly
280g (9 ounces) bottled artichoke hearts in brine, drained, halved
200g (6½ ounces) red grape tomatoes, halved
80g (2½ ounces) curly endive leaves
½ cup firmly packed fresh flat-leaf parsley leaves
herb and garlic dressing
2 tablespoons olive oil
2 tablespoons white wine vinegar
1 tablespoon lemon juice
1 tablespoon each finely chopped fresh basil and oregano
2 cloves garlic, chopped finely

1 Quarter capsicums; discard seeds and membranes. Roast capsicum, skin-side up, under hot grill (broiler) until skin blisters and blackens. Cover capsicum with plastic or paper for 5 minutes; peel away skin then cut pieces in half diagonally.
2 Meanwhile, cook chorizo in heated large frying pan, stirring, until browned. Drain on absorbent paper.
3 Make herb and garlic dressing.
4 Combine capsicum, chorizo, dressing and remaining ingredients in large bowl; season to taste.
herb and garlic dressing Combine ingredients in small bowl.

prep + cook time 25 minutes **serves** 4
nutritional count per serving 36g total fat (10.8g saturated fat); 1885kJ (451 cal); 16.4g carbohydrate; 20.5g protein; 3.9g fibre

Rib steaks with capsicum and almond salsa

8 x 250g (8-ounce) beef rib-eye (scotch fillet) steaks, bone in
1 teaspoon smoked paprika
capsicum and almond salsa
400g (12½ ounces) char-grilled red capsicum (bell pepper),
    chopped coarsely
½ cup (80g) almond kernels, roasted, chopped coarsely
1 small red onion (100g), chopped finely
1 cup (120g) seeded green olives, sliced thickly
1 cup coarsely chopped fresh flat-leaf parsley
½ cup coarsely chopped fresh oregano
2 fresh long red chillies, seeded, chopped finely
1 tablespoon extra virgin olive oil
1 tablespoon lemon juice
2 cloves garlic, crushed

1 Sprinkle both sides of beef with paprika; cook on heated oiled grill plate (or grill or barbecue) until browned both sides and cooked as desired. Remove from heat; cover, stand 10 minutes.
2 Meanwhile, make capsicum and almond salsa.
3 Serve beef with salsa.
capsicum and almond salsa Combine ingredients in medium bowl.

prep + cook time 45 minutes (+ standing) **serves** 8
nutritional count per serving 20g total fat (5.8g saturated fat);
1634kJ (391 cal); 6.9g carbohydrate; 44.7g protein; 2.4g fibre
tips Veal cutlets or pork cutlets can be used, if you prefer.
Char-grilled capsicum is available, in slices, from delicatessens, or bottled, in oil or brine, from many supermarkets.

Braised oxtails with orange

1.5kg (3 pounds) oxtails, cut into 5cm (2-inch) pieces
2 tablespoons plain (all-purpose) flour
2 tablespoons olive oil
1 medium brown onion (150g), chopped coarsely
2 cloves garlic, crushed
½ cup (125ml) sweet sherry
400g (12½ ounces) canned crushed tomatoes
1 cup (250ml) beef stock
1 cup (250ml) water
4 sprigs fresh thyme
2 dried bay leaves
10cm (4-inch) strip orange rind
4 medium tomatoes (600g), chopped coarsely
¼ cup finely chopped fresh flat-leaf parsley
1 tablespoon finely grated orange rind

1 Preheat oven to 160°C/325°F.
2 Coat oxtail in flour; shake off excess. Heat half the oil in large flameproof casserole dish; cook oxtail, in batches, until browned. Remove from pan.
3 Heat remaining oil in same dish; cook onion and garlic, stirring, until onion softens. Return oxtails to dish with sherry, undrained tomatoes, stock, the water, thyme, bay leaves and rind, cover; cook, in oven, about 3 hours or until oxtail is tender. Stir in chopped tomato; season to taste.
4 Serve oxtail sprinkled with parsley and rind.

prep + cook time 3 hour 30 minutes **serves** 4
nutritional count per serving 110.2g total fat (40g saturated fat); 5656kJ (1353 cal); 15.8g carbohydrate; 69.5g protein; 4.1g fibre
serving suggestion Mashed potato or steamed rice.

Chilli and citrus pork chops with orange watercress salad

¼ cup (60ml) lime juice
2 fresh small red thai (serrano) chillies, seeded, chopped finely
2 cloves garlic, crushed
½ cup (170g) orange marmalade
⅓ cup finely chopped fresh coriander (cilantro)
½ cup (125ml) tequila
8 pork loin chops (2.2kg)
orange watercress salad
2 large oranges (600g)
¼ cup (60ml) lime juice
¼ cup (85g) orange marmalade
2 tablespoons olive oil
2 teaspoons tequila
100g (3 ounces) watercress, trimmed
1 medium avocado (250g), sliced thinly
½ cup loosely packed fresh coriander (cilantro) leaves

1 Combine juice, chilli, garlic, marmalade, coriander, tequila and pork in large bowl. Cover; refrigerate overnight.
2 Make orange watercress salad.
3 Drain pork; reserve marinade. Cook pork on heated oiled grill plate (or grill or barbecue), brushing occasionally with marinade, until cooked as desired.
4 Serve pork with salad.
orange watercress salad Segment oranges over large bowl; stir in juice, marmalade and oil. Add remaining ingredients; toss gently to combine. Season to taste.

prep + cook time 30 minutes (+ refrigeration) **serves** 4
nutritional count per serving 25.2g total fat (5.5g saturated fat); 3461kJ (828 cal); 51.3g carbohydrate; 80.1g protein; 4.7g fibre

Grilled paprika veal and radicchio salad

600g (1¼ pounds) veal fillet
1 tablespoon olive oil
1 clove garlic, crushed
1 teaspoon finely grated lemon rind
½ teaspoon sweet paprika
2 medium radicchio (400g), trimmed, quartered
250g (8 ounces) red grape tomatoes, halved
1 medium yellow capsicum (bell pepper) (200g), chopped coarsely
1 small red onion (100g), sliced thinly
paprika mayonnaise
½ cup (150g) mayonnaise
1 tablespoon lemon juice
1 teaspoon sweet paprika

1 Combine veal, oil, garlic, rind and paprika in medium bowl. Cover; refrigerate 3 hours or overnight.
2 Make paprika mayonnaise.
3 Cook veal on heated oiled grill plate (or grill or barbecue) until cooked as desired. Cover veal; stand 5 minutes then slice thinly.
4 Meanwhile, cook radicchio on same heated oiled grill plate (or grill or barbecue) until heated through.
5 Place veal in medium bowl with remaining ingredients; toss gently to combine.
6 Divide radicchio among serving plates; top with veal mixture, drizzle with mayonnaise.
paprika mayonnaise Combine ingredients in small bowl; season to taste.

prep + cook time 20 minutes (+ refrigeration) **serves** 4
nutritional count per serving 19.4g total fat (2.6g saturated fat); 1584kJ (379 cal); 12.7g carbohydrate; 36.5g protein; 4.1g fibre

Braised veal shoulder with white beans

¼ cup (60ml) olive oil
1.2kg (2½-pound) boned veal shoulder, rolled, tied
2 medium brown onions (300g), sliced thickly
3 cloves garlic, crushed
½ cup (125ml) dry red wine
1 cinnamon stick
2 dried bay leaves
2 sprigs fresh rosemary
800g (1½ pounds) canned crushed tomatoes
½ cup (60g) seeded green olives
2 medium carrots (240g), chopped coarsely
½ cup (60g) frozen peas
400g (12½ ounces) canned white beans, rinsed, drained

1 Preheat oven to 200°C/400°F.
2 Heat 2 tablespoons of the oil in large flameproof baking dish; cook veal, turning, until browned all over. Remove from dish.
3 Heat remaining oil in same dish; cook onion and garlic, stirring, until onion softens. Add wine, cinnamon, bay leaves, rosemary, undrained tomatoes and olives; bring to the boil.
4 Return veal to dish; cover. Cook in oven 30 minutes. Turn veal and stir tomato mixture. Add carrots; cook, covered, 30 minutes.
5 Remove veal from dish; cover to keep warm. Add peas and beans to dish; cook, covered, 10 minutes. Season to taste.
6 Serve sliced veal with bean mixture.

prep + cook time 1 hour 40 minutes **serves** 6
nutritional count per serving 14.7g total fat (2.8g saturated fat); 1697kJ (406 cal); 12.7g carbohydrate; 49.2g protein; 5.4g fibre
tips Ask your butcher to bone, roll and tie the meat for you.
Many varieties of already cooked white beans are available canned, among them cannellini, butter and haricot beans; any of these are suitable for this stew.

Brown lentil, zucchini and chorizo salad

2 cured chorizo sausages (340g), sliced thinly
1 large zucchini (150g), sliced thinly lengthways
800g (1½ pounds) canned brown lentils, rinsed, drained
250g (8 ounces) red grape tomatoes, halved
1 cup loosely packed fresh flat-leaf parsley leaves
paprika dressing
2 teaspoons sweet smoked paprika
1 teaspoon ground cumin
¼ teaspoon chilli powder
¼ cup (60ml) olive oil
1 tablespoon red wine vinegar

1 Cook chorizo and zucchini on heated oiled grill plate (or grill or barbecue) until chorizo is browned and zucchini is tender.
2 Meanwhile, make paprika dressing.
3 Place chorizo, zucchini and dressing in large bowl with remaining ingredients; toss gently to combine. Season to taste.
paprika dressing Dry-fry spices in small frying pan until fragrant; cool. Place spices and remaining ingredients in screw-top jar; shake well.

prep + cook time 30 minutes **serves** 4
nutritional count per serving 39.8g total fat (11.2g saturated fat); 2161kJ (517 cal); 13.9g carbohydrate; 24.1g protein; 6.2g fibre

Paprika pork cutlets with carrot and olive salad

2 tablespoons olive oil
¼ cup (60ml) lemon juice
2 teaspoons ground cumin
1 tablespoon sweet paprika
4 pork cutlets (1kg)
carrot and olive salad
4 medium carrots (480g), halved lengthways, sliced thinly
1 cup (120g) seeded black olives, chopped coarsely
½ cup loosely packed fresh flat-leaf parsley leaves
½ cup loosely packed fresh coriander (cilantro) leaves
2 tablespoons olive oil
2 teaspoons ground cumin
1 tablespoon red wine vinegar

1 Combine oil, juice, cumin, paprika and pork in large bowl, season.
2 Cook pork on heated oiled grill plate (or grill or barbecue) until cooked as desired.
3 Meanwhile, make carrot and olive salad.
4 Serve pork with salad.
carrot and olive salad Boil, steam or microwave carrot until tender; drain. Cool 10 minutes. Place carrot in medium bowl with remaining ingredients; toss gently to combine.

prep + cook time 30 minutes **serves** 4
nutritional count per serving 24.8g total fat (4.8g saturated fat); 1718kJ (411 cal); 12.8g carbohydrate; 32.1g protein; 3.8g fibre

Lamb with aïoli

⅓ cup (80ml) olive oil
6 sprigs fresh thyme
900g (1¾ pounds) large potatoes
6 x 4 french-trimmed lamb
  cutlet racks (1kg)
500g (1 pound) spinach, trimmed
20g (¾ ounce) butter
250g (8 ounces) swiss brown
  mushrooms, sliced thickly
1 clove garlic, crushed
1 tablespoon balsamic vinegar

aïoli
½ teaspoon dijon mustard
1 tablespoon white wine vinegar
1 clove garlic, crushed
2 egg yolks
¾ cup (180ml) extra virgin olive oil
2 teaspoons lemon juice

1 Heat oil in small saucepan; deep-fry thyme, about 5 seconds or until fragrant. Drain on absorbent paper; reserve oil.

2 Preheat oven to 200°C/400°F.

3 Cut potatoes into 1cm (½-inch) slices. Heat 2 tablespoons of the reserved oil in flameproof baking dish; cook potato slices, in batches, until lightly browned both sides. Return potato to dish.

4 Add lamb to dish; roast about 20 minutes or until cooked as desired. Cover to keep warm.

5 Meanwhile, make aïoli.

6 Boil, steam or microwave spinach until wilted; drain.

7 Heat remaining reserved oil with butter in small saucepan; cook mushrooms and garlic, stirring, until mushrooms soften.

8 Cut each lamb rack into four cutlets; divide among serving plates with spinach, potato and mushrooms. Top with aïoli and fried thyme; drizzle with vinegar.

aïoli Whisk mustard, vinegar, garlic and egg yolks in small bowl until combined. Gradually add oil in thin, steady stream, whisking constantly, until mixture thickens. Whisk in juice.

prep + cook time 1 hour **serves** 6
nutritional count per serving 52.3g total fat (11.7g saturated fat); 2725kJ (652 cal); 17.2g carbohydrate; 26.3g protein; 5.4g fibre
tip Aïoli can be made up to 2 days ahead; store covered in the refrigerator.

Grilled lamb with paprikash sauce

800g (1½ pounds) lamb backstraps
1 tablespoon olive oil
1 small brown onion (80g), chopped finely
1 clove garlic, crushed
2 teaspoons sweet paprika
1 teaspoon smoked paprika
pinch cayenne pepper
400g (12½ ounces) canned crushed tomatoes
½ cup (125ml) water

1 Cook lamb on heated oiled grill plate (or grill or barbecue). Cover; stand 5 minutes then slice thickly.
2 Meanwhile, heat oil in medium saucepan; cook onion, stirring, until onion softens. Add garlic and spices; cook, stirring, about 1 minute or until fragrant.
3 Add undrained tomatoes and the water; bring to the boil. Reduce heat; simmer, uncovered, about 5 minutes or until sauce thickens slightly.
4 Serve lamb with paprikash sauce.

prep + cook time 15 minutes **serves** 4
nutritional count per serving 12g total fat (3.8g saturated fat); 1241kJ (297 cal); 4.4g carbohydrate; 42.1g protein; 1.6g fibre
serving suggestion Baked potatoes.

Vegetables

Gazpacho

1kg (2 pounds) ripe tomatoes, peeled, chopped coarsely
2 lebanese cucumbers (260g), seeded, chopped coarsely
2 large red capsicums (bell peppers) (700g), chopped coarsely
1 large green capsicum (bell pepper) (350g), chopped coarsely
1 large red onion (200g), chopped coarsely
2 cloves garlic, chopped coarsely
1⅔ cups (410ml) canned tomato juice
2 tablespoons red wine vinegar
1 tablespoon olive oil
2 teaspoons Tabasco
1 medium avocado (250g), chopped finely
1 small yellow capsicum (bell pepper) (150g), chopped finely
¼ cup finely chopped fresh coriander (cilantro)

1 Blend or process tomato, cucumber, capsicums, onion, garlic, juice, vinegar, oil and Tabasco, in batches, until smooth. Pour into large jug. Cover; refrigerate 3 hours.
2 Stir soup; season to taste. Pour soup into serving bowls; top with remaining ingredients. Serve gazpacho sprinkled with extra Tabasco, if you like.

prep time 25 minutes (+ refrigeration) **serves** 6
nutritional count per serving 10.4g total fat (1.9g saturated fat); 786kJ (188 cal); 14.5g carbohydrate; 6.2g protein; 6.3g fibre

Chilli tomato

¼ cup coarsely chopped fresh flat-leaf parsley
2 cloves garlic, crushed
½ teaspoon dried chilli flakes
2 tablespoons olive oil
4 large egg (plum) tomatoes (360g), sliced thickly

1 Combine parsley, garlic and chilli in small bowl.
2 Heat oil in large frying pan, carefully add tomato in a single layer; cook, over high heat, 2 minutes. Turn tomato, sprinkle with parsley mixture; cook, shaking pan occasionally, about 1 minute or until tomato is caramelised but still holding its shape.
3 Transfer to serving plate; drizzle with pan juices. Season to taste.

prep + cook time 15 minutes **serves** 6
nutritional count per serving 6.2g total fat (0.9g saturated fat); 276kJ (66 cal); 1.5g carbohydrate; 0.7g protein; 1.1g fibre
tips Take care when adding tomato to pan as it may splatter. Tomato is best cooked just before serving.
Although delicious on its own (or as part of a tapas spread), this dish also goes well with roasted meat and poultry or served with a green salad and some shaved manchego (or parmesan) cheese.

Cheese and tomato tortilla

4 green onions (scallions), sliced thickly
1 medium red capsicum (bell pepper) (200g), chopped coarsely
2 cloves garlic, crushed
1 fresh long red chilli, chopped finely
2 medium tomatoes (300g), chopped coarsely
200g (6½ ounces) fetta cheese, crumbled
8 eggs
1¼ cups (310ml) pouring cream
¼ cup firmly packed fresh flat-leaf parsley leaves, chopped coarsely

1 Heat oiled 26cm (10½-inch) frying pan; cook onion, capsicum, garlic and chilli, stirring, until vegetables are tender. Remove from heat; stir in tomato and cheese.
2 Whisk eggs, cream and parsley in large jug, season. Pour over capsicum mixture; stir gently.
3 Preheat grill (broiler).
4 Return pan to low heat; cook tortilla, uncovered, until just set. Place pan under grill to brown tortilla top. Cut into wedges to serve.

prep + cook time 35 minutes **serves** 4
nutritional count per serving 49.9g total fat (29g saturated fat); 2424kJ (580 cal); 7.6g carbohydrate; 25.6g protein; 2.2g fibre
tips We used a goat's milk fetta cheese.
It is fine to use just one 300ml carton of cream for this recipe.
Wrap the handle of your frying pan with foil to protect it, if necessary.

Vegetable paella

1 tablespoon olive oil
1 small red onion (100g), chopped finely
1 medium red capsicum (bell pepper) (200g), chopped finely
1 medium yellow capsicum (bell pepper) (200g), chopped finely
1 teaspoon smoked paprika
200g (6½ ounces) swiss brown mushrooms, halved
1⅔ cups (330g) brown short-grain rice
pinch saffron threads
4 medium tomatoes (600g), chopped coarsely
1 litre (4 cups) vegetable stock
200g (6½ ounces) green beans, trimmed, chopped coarsely
1 cup (120g) frozen peas
2 tablespoons coarsely chopped fresh flat-leaf parsley
1 medium lemon (140g), cut into wedges

1 Heat oil in large deep frying pan; cook onion and capsicums, stirring, until onion softens. Add paprika and mushrooms; cook, stirring, until mushrooms are tender. Add rice and saffron; stir to coat rice in vegetable mixture.
2 Add tomato and 1 cup of the stock; cook, stirring, until liquid is absorbed. Add remaining stock; cook, covered, stirring occasionally, about 1 hour or until liquid is absorbed and rice is tender.
3 Sprinkle beans and peas over rice (do not stir to combine). Cook, covered, about 10 minutes or until beans are tender. Season to taste.
4 Cover paella; stand 5 minutes. Sprinkle paella with parsley; serve with lemon wedges.

prep + cook time 1 hour 40 minutes **serves** 6
nutritional count per serving 5.5g total fat (1g saturated fat); 1333kJ (319 cal); 51.2g carbohydrate; 11.4g protein; 7.4g fibre

Chickpea, tomato and capsicum salad

⅓ cup (80ml) olive oil
3 medium red capsicums (bell pepper) (600g), sliced thinly
2 cloves garlic, crushed
¼ cup (60ml) lemon juice
2 tablespoons red wine vinegar
400g (12½ ounces) canned chickpeas, rinsed, drained
4 small tomatoes (360g), sliced thinly
1 cup coarsely chopped fresh flat-leaf parsley

1 Heat half the oil in large frying pan; cook capsicum and garlic, stirring, about 5 minutes or until capsicum softens. Cool.
2 Place capsicum mixture in large bowl with remaining oil, juice, vinegar, chickpeas, tomato and parsley; toss gently to combine. Season to taste.

prep + cook time 20 minutes (+ cooling) **serves** 8
nutritional count per serving 10g total fat (1.4g saturated fat); 606kJ (145 cal); 8.2g carbohydrate; 3.8g protein; 3.3g fibre
serving suggestion Lemon wedges.

Valencian salad

6 large oranges (1.8kg), peeled, sliced thinly
2 medium tomatoes (300g), sliced thickly
1 large red onion (300g), sliced thinly
100g (3 ounces) manchego cheese, shaved
¾ cup (120g) seeded black olives, halved
2 large avocados (640g), chopped coarsely
1 cup loosely packed fresh mint leaves
orange dressing
2 tablespoons olive oil
2 tablespoons red wine vinegar
2 tablespoons orange juice
1 clove garlic, crushed

1 Make orange dressing.
2 Place orange in large bowl with remaining ingredients and dressing; toss gently to combine. Season to taste.
orange dressing Place ingredients in screw-top jar; shake well.

prep time 20 minutes **serves** 6
nutritional count per serving 28.9g total fat (8g saturated fat); 1743kJ (417 cal); 25.3g carbohydrate; 11g protein; 6.7g fibre
tip Manchego cheese is a sharp, firm Spanish cheese; it can be found in most specialty food stores and delicatessens. You can use parmesan cheese instead, if manchego is not available.

Stuffed capsicums

2 teaspoons olive oil
1 medium red onion (170g), chopped finely
1 tablespoon slivered almonds
⅔ cup (130g) white long-grain rice
1 cup (250ml) water
2 tablespoons finely chopped dried apricots
¼ cup (35g) sun-dried tomatoes, chopped finely
¼ cup finely chopped fresh flat-leaf parsley
4 medium red capsicums (bell peppers) (800g)
cooking-oil spray
roasted tomato salad
2 medium tomatoes (300g), cut into thick wedges
1 tablespoon cider vinegar
½ teaspoon cracked black pepper
1 teaspoon white (granulated) sugar
1 cup firmly packed fresh flat-leaf parsley leaves
½ cup firmly packed fresh mint leaves

1 Preheat oven to 200°C/400°F.
2 Heat oil in medium saucepan; cook onion and nuts, stirring, until onion softens. Add rice; cook, stirring, 1 minute. Add the water; bring to the boil. Reduce heat; simmer, covered, 15 minutes or until liquid is absorbed and rice is tender. Stir in apricot, tomato and parsley; season to taste.
3 Carefully cut tops off capsicums; discard tops. Discard seeds and membranes, leaving capsicum intact. Spoon rice mixture into capsicums; place capsicums on oven tray, spray with oil. Roast 10 minutes. Cover loosely with foil; roast about 20 minutes or until capsicums are just soft.
4 Meanwhile, make roasted tomato salad.
5 Serve capsicums with roasted tomato salad.
roasted tomato salad Combine tomato, vinegar, pepper and sugar in medium bowl. Drain; reserve liquid. Place tomato on oven tray; roast, alongside capsicums, 10 minutes or until tomato just softens. Place tomato and reserved liquid in medium bowl with herbs; toss gently to combine.

prep + cook time 1 hour 15 minutes **serves** 4
nutritional count per serving 5.7g total fat (0.6g saturated fat); 1087kJ (260 cal); 43.4g carbohydrate; 8.2g protein; 7.3g fibre

Tortilla with tomato salsa

2 large potatoes (600g), sliced thinly
2 medium brown onions (300g), sliced thinly
1 medium red capsicum (bell pepper) (200g), chopped coarsely
150g (4½ ounces) green beans, trimmed, chopped coarsely
8 eggs
¼ cup (60ml) skim milk
⅓ cup coarsely chopped fresh flat-leaf parsley
tomato salsa
1 large tomato (220g), seeded, chopped finely
2 lebanese cucumbers (260g), seeded, chopped finely
1 small red onion (100g), chopped finely
2 long green chillies, chopped finely
¼ cup (60ml) lemon juice
2 tablespoons finely chopped fresh coriander (cilantro)

1 Heat oiled 26cm (10½-inch) frying pan; cook potato and onion, stirring, 2 minutes. Reduce heat; cook, covered, stirring occasionally, 15 minutes. Add capsicum and beans; cook, covered, about 5 minutes or until potato is tender. Remove from heat.
2 Whisk eggs, milk and parsley in large jug, season. Pour egg mixture over potato mixture; stir gently.
3 Return pan to low heat; cook, uncovered, 20 minutes. Cover; cook about 10 minutes or until tortilla is set.
4 Meanwhile, make tomato salsa.
5 Serve tortilla topped with salsa.
tomato salsa Combine ingredients in small bowl.

prep + cook time 1 hour 15 minutes **serves** 6
nutritional count per serving 7.4g total fat (2.2g saturated fat); 1672kJ (200 cal); 18.7g carbohydrate; 14.1g protein; 4.5g fibre

Roasted capsicum and beetroot salad

500g (1 pound) baby beetroot (beets)
1 small red capsicum (bell pepper) (150g)
1 small orange capsicum (bell pepper) (150g)
1 small yellow capsicum (bell pepper) (150g)
cooking-oil spray
½ small red onion (50g), chopped finely
1 tablespoon finely chopped fresh flat-leaf parsley
1 tablespoon thinly sliced preserved lemon rind
1 tablespoon lemon juice

1 Preheat oven to 220°C/425°F.
2 Trim leaves from beetroot; wrap each beetroot in foil, place on oven tray. Place capsicums on baking-paper-lined oven tray; spray with oil. Roast beetroot and capsicums about 30 minutes or until beetroot are tender and capsicums have blistered and blackened.
3 Cool beetroot 10 minutes then peel and quarter. Cover capsicums with plastic or paper for 5 minutes. Quarter capsicums; discard seeds and membranes. Peel away skin, then halve each quarter lengthways.
4 Arrange beetroot and capsicum on large serving platter. Sprinkle with onion, parsley and preserved lemon; drizzle with juice, season to taste.

prep + cook time 50 minutes **serves** 4
nutritional count per serving 1.6g total fat (0.2g saturated fat); 397kJ (95 cal); 13.9g carbohydrate; 3.9g protein; 4.8g fibre

Orange and radish salad

10 trimmed medium red radishes (150g), sliced thinly
4 large oranges (1.2kg), segmented
1 small red onion (100g), sliced thinly
2 tablespoons each coarsely chopped fresh flat-leaf parsley and
    coriander (cilantro)
¼ cup (60ml) orange juice

1 Arrange radish, orange and onion on serving platter; sprinkle with parsley and coriander, drizzle with juice.
2 Cover salad; refrigerate 1 hour before serving.

prep time 20 minutes (+ refrigeration) **serves** 4
nutritional count per serving 0.3g total fat (0g saturated fat);
447kJ (107 cal); 20.1g carbohydrate; 3g protein; 5.2g fibre

Cream of roasted garlic and potato soup

2 medium garlic bulbs (140g), unpeeled
2 tablespoons olive oil
2 medium brown onions (300g), chopped coarsely
1 tablespoon fresh thyme leaves
5 medium potatoes (1kg), chopped coarsely
1.25 litres (5 cups) chicken stock
¾ cup (180ml) pouring cream

1 Preheat oven to 180°C/350°F.
2 Separate garlic bulbs into cloves; place unpeeled cloves, in single layer, on oven tray. Drizzle with half the oil. Roast about 15 minutes or until garlic is soft. When cool enough to handle, squeeze garlic into small bowl, discard skins.
3 Meanwhile, heat remaining oil in large saucepan; cook onion and thyme, stirring, until onion softens. Add potato; cook, stirring, 5 minutes. Add stock; bring to the boil. Reduce heat; simmer, uncovered, about 15 minutes or until potato is tender. Stir in garlic; simmer, uncovered, 5 minutes.
4 Blend or process soup (or pass through a food mill [mouli] or fine sieve), in batches, until smooth then return to pan. Reheat until hot then stir in cream; season to taste. Divide soup among serving bowls; sprinkle with extra thyme, if you like.

prep + cook time 40 minutes **serves** 4
nutritional count per serving 27.9g total fat (13g saturated fat); 1864kJ (446 cal); 36.8g carbohydrate; 12g protein; 8.5g fibre
tip Garlic's cooking times make a huge difference to its pungency: the longer it's cooked, the more creamy in texture and subtly nutty in flavour it becomes.

Cauliflower with garlic, chilli and anchovies

2kg (4 pounds) cauliflower, cut into small florets
1/3 cup (80ml) extra virgin olive oil
2 fresh long red chillies, seeded, chopped finely
4 cloves garlic, chopped finely
6 drained anchovy fillets, chopped finely
1 cup coarsely chopped fresh flat-leaf parsley
2 tablespoons lemon juice
1 medium lemon (140g), cut into wedges

1 Boil, steam or microwave cauliflower until almost tender; drain well.
2 Heat oil in large deep frying pan; cook chilli, garlic and anchovy, stirring, until fragrant. Add cauliflower; cook, stirring, until hot. Remove from heat; stir in parsley and juice. Season to taste. Serve with lemon wedges.

prep + cook time 40 minutes **serves** 8
nutritional count per serving 9.8g total fat (1.3g saturated fat); 614kJ (147 cal); 5.6g carbohydrate; 6.6g protein; 5.1g fibre
tip If you don't have a large frying pan, toss the cauliflower with the anchovy mixture in a wok.

Lemon, garlic and chilli potatoes

1kg (2 pounds) baby new potatoes, unpeeled,
    cut into 1cm (½-inch) slices
½ cup coarsely chopped fresh flat-leaf parsley
¼ cup coarsely chopped fresh chives
lemon and chilli butter
100g (3 ounces) butter, softened
2 cloves garlic, crushed
1 tablespoon finely grated lemon rind
1 teaspoon dried chilli flakes

1 Make lemon and chilli butter.
2 Boil, steam or microwave potato until tender; drain.
3 Combine hot potato, lemon and chilli butter, parsley and chives in large bowl; season to taste.
lemon and chilli butter Combine ingredients in small bowl.

prep + cook time 30 minutes **serves** 8
nutritional count per serving 10.4g total fat (6.8g saturated fat);
744kJ (178 cal); 16.6g carbohydrate; 3.2g protein; 2.9g fibre

Char-grilled vegetables with oregano dressing

1 medium red capsicum (bell pepper) (200g)
1 medium yellow capsicum (bell pepper) (200g)
1 large red onion (300g), halved, cut into wedges
1 small kumara (orange sweet potato) (250g), sliced thinly lengthways
2 baby eggplants (120g), sliced thinly lengthways
2 medium zucchini (240g), halved lengthways
280g (9 ounces) bottled artichoke hearts, drained, halved
¾ cup (90g) seeded black olives
1 small radicchio (150g), trimmed, leaves separated
oregano dressing
¼ cup (60ml) olive oil
2 tablespoons red wine vinegar
2 tablespoons lemon juice
2 cloves garlic, crushed
1 tablespoon finely chopped fresh oregano

1 Quarter capsicums; remove seeds and membranes. Cut capsicum into thick strips. Cook capsicum, in batches, on heated oiled grill plate (or grill or barbecue) until browned and tender.
2 Cook onion, kumara, eggplant, zucchini and artichoke, in batches, on same grill plate (or grill or barbecue) until browned.
3 Meanwhile, make oregano dressing.
4 Place char-grilled vegetables in large bowl with olives and dressing; toss gently to combine. Season to taste. Serve with radicchio.
oregano dressing Place ingredients in screw-top jar; shake well.

prep + cook time 55 minutes **serves** 4
nutritional count per serving 14.8g total fat (2g saturated fat); 1104kJ (264 cal); 22.8g carbohydrate; 6.4g protein; 7.6g fibre
tip This robust salad can be made ahead with great success: the flavours of the dressing's fresh oregano and lemon will permeate the grilled vegetables and make them even more delicious.

Three bean salad with lemon chilli crumbs

150g (4½ ounces) green beans, trimmed
150g (4½ ounces) yellow beans, trimmed
300g (9½ ounces) frozen broad beans (fava beans)
2 tablespoons olive oil
2 tablespoons lemon juice
lemon chilli crumbs
25g (¾ ounce) butter
1 tablespoon finely grated lemon rind
⅓ cup (25g) stale breadcrumbs
¼ teaspoon chilli powder

1 Make lemon chilli crumbs.
2 Boil, steam or microwave green, yellow and broad beans, separately, until tender; drain. Rinse under cold water; drain. Peel away grey outer shells from broad beans.
3 Place all beans in medium bowl with oil and juice; toss gently to combine. Season to taste. Sprinkle with crumbs.
lemon chilli crumbs Melt butter in small frying pan; cook remaining ingredients over low heat, stirring, until crumbs are browned.

prep + cook time 25 minutes **serves** 6
nutritional count per serving 10g total fat (3.2g saturated fat); 594kJ (142 cal); 5.3g carbohydrate; 5.2g protein; 4.8g fibre

Roasted capsicum and goat's cheese salad

2 medium orange capsicums (bell peppers) (400g)
2 medium red capsicums (bell peppers) (400g)
2 medium yellow capsicums (bell peppers) (400g)
2 medium green capsicums (bell peppers) (400g)
80g (2½ ounces) baby rocket leaves (arugula)
1 small red onion (100g), sliced thinly
240g (7½ ounces) goat's cheese, crumbled
oregano vinaigrette
⅓ cup (80ml) olive oil
2 tablespoons red wine vinegar
1 clove garlic, crushed
1 tablespoon finely chopped fresh oregano

1 Preheat oven to 200°C/400°F.
2 Quarter capsicums; discard seeds and membranes. Place, skin-side up, on oven tray. Roast about 20 minutes or until skin blisters and blackens. Cover capsicum pieces with plastic or paper for 5 minutes; peel away skin, then slice capsicum thickly.
3 Make oregano vinaigrette.
4 Place capsicum in large bowl with rocket and onion; toss gently to combine. Sprinkle with cheese, drizzle with vinaigrette.
oregano vinaigrette Place ingredients in screw-top jar; shake well. Season to taste.

prep + cook time 30 minutes **serves** 4
nutritional count per serving 28.5g total fat (8.8g saturated fat); 1605kJ (384 cal); 15.9g carbohydrate; 14.2g protein; 4.6g fibre

Cabbage, orange and radish salad

1 medium orange (240g) —
2 cups (160g) finely shredded green cabbage
2 red radishes (70g), trimmed, sliced thinly
½ cup loosely packed fresh mint leaves
cumin and orange dressing
1 teaspoon cumin seeds
¼ teaspoon hot paprika
2 tablespoons olive oil
1 tablespoon white balsamic vinegar

1 Segment orange over small bowl; reserve 1 tablespoon juice for dressing.
2 Make cumin and orange dressing.
3 Place orange segments in large bowl with dressing and remaining ingredients; toss gently to combine. Season to taste.
cumin and orange dressing Dry-fry spices in heated small frying pan until fragrant; cool. Place spices in screw-top jar with oil, vinegar and reserved orange juice; shake well.

prep + cook time 25 minutes **serves** 4
nutritional count per serving 9.3g total fat (1.3g saturated fat); 472kJ (113 cal); 5g carbohydrate; 1.3g protein; 2.9g fibre

Ruby grapefruit, pomegranate and endive salad

3 ruby red grapefruit (1kg)
¼ cup (60ml) olive oil
2 tablespoons coarsely chopped fresh chervil
100g (3 ounces) curly endive leaves
½ cup (125ml) pomegranate pulp
½ cup (55g) coarsely chopped walnuts, roasted

1 Juice half of one grapefruit; reserve juice. Peel remaining grapefruit; slice thickly.
2 Place reserved juice in screw-top jar with oil and chervil; shake well.
3 Place endive in large bowl with dressing; toss gently to combine. Season to taste.
4 Arrange endive, grapefruit and pomegranate on serving plate; serve sprinkled with nuts.

prep time 15 minutes **serves** 4
nutritional count per serving 23.7g total fat (2.5g saturated fat); 1208kJ (289 cal); 12.8g carbohydrate; 4.5g protein; 4.6g fibre
tip You need 1 medium pomegranate for this recipe. Pomegranate pulp consists of the seeds and the edible pulp surrounding them; it has a tangy sweet-sour flavour. To remove the seeds, cut the fruit in half crossways and hold each half cut-side down over a bowl. Hit the outside skin of the fruit sharply with a wooden spoon – as hard as you can – the seeds should fall out – if they don't, dig them out with a teaspoon.

Barbecued corn, broad beans and capsicum

4 trimmed corn cobs (1kg)
500g (1 pound) frozen broad beans (fava beans)
1 medium red capsicum (bell pepper) (200g), chopped finely
1 tablespoon olive oil

1 Cook corn on heated oiled grill plate (or grill or barbecue) until tender.
When cool enough to handle, use a sharp knife to cut kernels from cobs.
2 Meanwhile, boil, steam or microwave broad beans until tender; drain.
Peel away grey outer shells from broad beans.
3 Place corn and beans in large bowl with remaining ingredients;
toss gently to combine. Season to taste.

prep + cook time 35 minutes **serves** 8
nutritional count per serving 3.2g total fat (1.5g saturated fat);
527kJ (126 cal); 16.4g carbohydrate; 5.1g protein; 5.2g fibre

Artichokes in oregano vinaigrette

6 medium globe artichokes (1.2kg)
½ cup (125ml) lemon juice
⅓ cup (80ml) olive oil
1 tablespoon white wine vinegar
2 cloves garlic, crushed
1 small red onion (100g), sliced thinly
1 tablespoon fresh oregano leaves

1 Prepare artichokes by snapping off tough outer leaves and peeling stems. Trim stems to 5cm (2 inches). Cut 2cm (¾ inch) off top of artichokes to reveal chokes. Cut artichokes in quarters from top to bottom, then scoop out and discard furry chokes from centres. As you finish preparing each artichoke, place it in a large bowl of water containing half the juice (this stops any discolouration while you are preparing the next one).
2 Add artichoke and remaining juice to large saucepan of boiling water; boil, uncovered, about 20 minutes or until tender. Drain; cool.
3 Place artichokes in large bowl; pour over combined oil, vinegar and garlic. Cover; refrigerate 3 hours or overnight.
4 Combine artichoke mixture with onion; season to taste. Serve sprinkled with oregano.

prep + cook time 1 hour (+ refrigeration) **serves** 6
nutritional count per serving 12.5g total fat (1.7g saturated fat); 694kJ (166 cal); 3.3g carbohydrate; 4.2g protein; 11.3g fibre

Chickpea, garlic and mint soup

2 teaspoons olive oil
2 medium brown onions (300g), chopped coarsely
5 cloves garlic, crushed
1 teaspoon ground cumin
2 litres (8 cups) chicken stock
2 tablespoons white wine vinegar
800g (1 ½ pounds) canned chickpeas (garbanzo beans),
   rinsed, drained
2 large tomatoes (440g), seeded, chopped finely
2 tablespoons finely shredded fresh mint

1 Heat oil in large saucepan; cook onion and garlic, stirring, until softened. Add cumin; cook, stirring, until fragrant. Add stock and vinegar; bring to the boil. Add chickpeas; simmer, uncovered, 15 minutes.
2 Add tomato; simmer, uncovered, about 5 minutes or until tomato is soft. Season to taste.
3 Serve soup sprinkled with mint.

prep + cook time 35 minutes **serves** 6
nutritional count per serving 4.9g total fat (1.2g saturated fat); 698kJ (167 cal); 18g carbohydrate; 10.5g protein; 5.7g fibre
serving suggestion Crusty white bread.

Olive and capsicum brown rice

2 cups (400g) brown medium-grain rice
2 large red capsicums (bell peppers) (700g)
1 cup (160g) fetta-stuffed green olives, sliced thinly
1 tablespoon finely chopped fresh oregano
1 fresh long red chilli, chopped finely
red wine vinaigrette
2 tablespoons lemon juice
2 tablespoons red wine vinegar
2 tablespoons olive oil
½ teaspoon white (granulated) sugar
1 clove garlic, crushed

1 Cook rice in large saucepan of boiling water, uncovered, until tender; drain. Rinse under cold water; drain. Place in large bowl.
2 Meanwhile, quarter capsicums; discard seeds and membranes. Cook capsicum, skin-side up, under hot grill (broiler) until skin blisters and blackens. Cover capsicum with paper or plastic for 5 minutes; peel away skin then slice thinly.
3 Make red wine vinaigrette.
4 Add capsicum, vinaigrette and remaining ingredients to rice; season to taste, mix gently.
red wine vinaigrette Place ingredients in screw-top jar; shake well.

prep + cook time 40 minutes **serves** 8
nutritional count per serving 7.6g total fat (1.1g saturated fat); 1120kJ (268 cal); 42.5g carbohydrate; 5.3g protein; 4.1g fibre

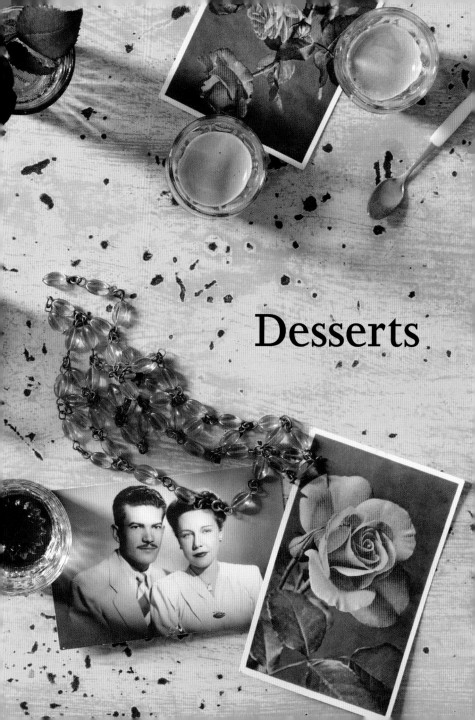

Desserts

Hot chocolate

1 litre (4 cups) milk
3 x 5cm (2-inch) strips orange rind
1 cinnamon stick
185g (6 ounces) dark eating (semi-sweet) chocolate, chopped finely

1 Bring milk, rind and cinnamon to the boil in medium saucepan.
Remove from heat; stand, covered, 5 minutes.
2 Discard rind and cinnamon. Add chocolate; stir until smooth.

prep + cook time 15 minutes (+ standing) **serves** 6
nutritional count per serving 15.3g total fat (9.5g saturated fat);
1133kJ (271 cal); 27.4g carbohydrate; 7.2g protein; 0.4g fibre

Crema catalana

8 egg yolks
1 cup (220g) caster (superfine) sugar
1.125 litres (4½ cups) milk
2 teaspoons finely grated lemon rind
1 cinnamon stick
½ cup (75g) cornflour (cornstarch)
⅓ cup (75g) caster (superfine) sugar, extra

1 Whisk egg yolks and sugar in large bowl until creamy.
2 Stir 1 litre (4 cup) of the milk, rind and cinnamon in large saucepan over medium heat until mixture just comes to the boil. Remove immediately from heat.
3 Strain milk into large heatproof jug; gradually whisk milk mixture into egg mixture. Blend cornflour with remaining milk in small jug; whisk into egg mixture.
4 Return mixture to pan; cook, stirring, until mixture boils and thickens.
5 Pour mixture into 26cm (10½-inch) heatproof pie dish; cover, refrigerate 4 hours or overnight.
6 Just before serving, sprinkle with extra sugar; cook under preheated grill (broiler) until sugar is caramelised.

prep + cook time 25 minutes (+ refrigeration) **serves** 8
nutritional count per serving 7g total fat (4.2g saturated fat); 903kJ (216 cal); 52.2g carbohydrate; 5.6g protein; 0g fibre

Olive oil cake

3 eggs
1 cup (220g) caster (superfine) sugar
1 tablespoon finely grated orange rind
2¼ cups (335g) self-raising flour
¼ cup (60ml) orange juice
½ cup (125ml) skim milk
1 cup (250ml) extra virgin olive oil
½ cup (125ml) orange juice, warmed, extra
¼ cup (40g) icing (confectioners') sugar

1 Preheat oven to 200°C/400°F. Oil deep 22cm (9-inch) square cake pan.
2 Beat eggs, caster sugar and rind in medium bowl with electric mixer until thick and creamy and sugar is dissolved. Stir in sifted flour, then combined juice, milk and oil, in three batches. Pour mixture into pan.
3 Bake cake about 45 minutes. Stand cake in pan 5 minutes; turn, top-side up, onto wire rack placed over tray.
4 Pour extra juice over hot cake; dust with sifted icing sugar. Cool cake before serving.

prep + cook time 1 hour 10 minutes **serves** 10
nutritional count per serving 24.8g total fat (3.8g saturated fat); 1526kJ (365 cal); 51.8g carbohydrate; 5.9g protein; 1.3g fibre
tip Lemon rind and juice can be substituted for the orange.

Almond turron

2 sheets confectioners' rice paper
3 cups (480g) blanched almonds, roasted
½ cup (175g) honey
1⅓ cups (300g) caster (superfine) sugar
2 tablespoons water
1 egg white

1 Grease 8cm x 26cm (3-inch x 10½-inch) bar cake pan. Line base and long sides with baking paper, extending paper 5cm (2 inches) over long sides. Place one sheet of rice paper in pan, covering base and up long sides.
2 Stir honey, sugar and the water in small saucepan over low heat until sugar dissolves. Using pastry brush dipped in water, brush down side of pan to dissolve all sugar crystals. Bring syrup to the boil; boil, uncovered, without stirring, about 10 minutes or until syrup reaches 164°C (327°C) on candy thermometer. Remove from heat.
3 Just before syrup is ready, beat egg white in small heatproof bowl with electric mixer until soft peaks form. With motor operating, add hot syrup to egg white in thin, steady stream. Beat until all syrup is added and mixture thickens.
4 Working quickly, transfer egg white mixture to large bowl; stir in nuts. Spoon mixture into pan; press firmly. Trim remaining sheet of rice paper to fit top of nougat; press on lightly, smoothing surface. Stand 2 hours or until cooled to room temperature and firm, before cutting.

prep + cook time 35 minutes (+ standing) **makes** 25
nutritional count per piece 10.6g total fat (0.7g saturated fat); 777kJ (186 cal); 18.8g carbohydrate; 4g protein; 1.7g fibre
tips A candy thermometer, available from kitchenware stores, is essential for this recipe. Place thermometer in large saucepan of simmering water while syrup is heating. This will stop thermometer cracking when placed in hot syrup. Once syrup is at correct temperature, return thermometer to pan of water; remove from heat. When cool, rinse and dry. You will need a powerful electric mixer. Standing mixers generally have more powerful motors than most hand-held electric mixers. Rice paper is edible and ready to use. It can be bought from specialty food stores; don't confuse this paper with the rice paper used in "rice paper rolls" which needs soaking to soften. Use a lightly oiled knife to cut turron. Turron can be made a week ahead; store in airtight container in a cool, dry place. Do not refrigerate.

Cinnamon flan

1 cup (220g) caster (superfine) sugar
½ cup (125ml) water
2½ cups (625ml) milk
1¼ cups (310ml) thickened (heavy) cream
2 cinnamon sticks
2 cloves
4 eggs
2 egg yolks
⅓ cup (75g) caster (superfine) sugar, extra
2 teaspoons vanilla extract

1 Preheat oven to 160°C/325°F.
2 Stir sugar and the water in medium saucepan over low heat until sugar dissolves; bring to the boil. Reduce heat; simmer, uncovered, without stirring, until mixture is golden brown in colour. Pour toffee into deep 20cm (8-inch) round cake pan. Place pan in large baking dish.
3 Bring milk, cream and spices to the boil in medium saucepan. Remove from heat; stand, covered, 15 minutes. Strain milk mixture into large heatproof jug; discard spices.
4 Whisk eggs, egg yolks, extra sugar and extract in medium bowl. Gradually whisk milk mixture into egg mixture; strain mixture over toffee in pan. Add enough boiling water to baking dish to come halfway up side of pan. Bake about 45 minutes or until custard sets. Remove pan from water; cool. Cover; refrigerate 24 hours.
5 Just before serving, turn flan onto a rimmed serving dish.

prep + cook time 1 hour 15 minutes (+ standing & refrigeration)
serves 8
nutritional count per serving 21.5g total fat (12.8g saturated fat); 1154kJ (276 cal); 42g carbohydrate; 7.6g protein; 0g fibre
tips This recipe must be made 24 hours in advance to allow the toffee to dissolve.
It is fine to use just one 300ml carton of cream in this recipe.

Honey-wine pastries

2 cups (300g) plain (all-purpose) flour
½ teaspoon ground cinnamon
½ teaspoon finely grated lemon rind
⅓ cup (80ml) light olive oil
⅔ cup (160ml) sweet dessert wine
vegetable oil, for deep-frying
1 tablespoon icing (confectioners') sugar
½ cup (180g) honey
½ teaspoon whole cloves
1 cinnamon stick
2 star anise

1 Sift flour and ground cinnamon into medium bowl; stir in rind, oil and wine to form a soft dough. Knead dough on floured surface until smooth. Cover with plastic wrap; stand 30 minutes.
2 Divide pastry in half; roll each piece between sheets of baking paper until 5mm (¼-inch) thick. Cut 5cm (2-inch) fluted rounds from pastry; re-rolling scraps and resting the pastry between each rolling, if necessary.
3 Heat oil in large saucepan; deep-fry pastries, in batches, until browned lightly. Drain on absorbent paper; dust with sifted icing sugar.
4 Meanwhile, bring honey, cloves, cinnamon stick and star anise to the boil in small saucepan. Boil, uncovered, 2 minutes. Strain syrup into a small heatproof jug; discard spices. Cool 5 minutes.
5 Transfer pastries to plate, drizzle with syrup.

prep + cook time 35 minutes (+ standing) **makes** 36
nutritional count per pastry 2.1g total fat (0.3g saturated fat); 297kJ (71 cal); 11g carbohydrate; 0.9g protein; 0.3g fibre
tips We used a sauternes-style dessert wine for this recipe.
We used a 5cm (2-inch) fluted round cutter. You could also use a 5cm (2-inch) fluted square cutter or a fluted pastry cutter wheel to cut squares from pastry.

Fried milk

2½ cups (625ml) milk
1 cinnamon stick
2 x 5cm (2-inch) strips orange rind
2 eggs
1 egg yolk
⅓ cup (50g) plain (all-purpose) flour
¼ cup (35g) cornflour (cornstarch)
1 teaspoon vanilla extract
½ cup (110g) caster (superfine) sugar
¼ cup (35g) plain (all-purpose) flour, extra
vegetable oil, for deep-frying
½ cup (110g) caster (superfine) sugar, extra
½ teaspoon ground cinnamon

1 Grease 20cm x 30cm (8-inch x 12-inch) rectangular slice pan. Line base and long sides with baking paper, extending paper 5cm (2 inches) over long sides.
2 Bring milk, cinnamon stick and rind to the boil in medium saucepan. Remove from heat; stand, covered, 10 minutes. Discard cinnamon stick and rind.
3 Whisk eggs, egg yolk, flours, extract and sugar in medium bowl until smooth. Gradually whisk egg mixture into warm milk mixture; cook, stirring, until custard boils and thickens. Reduce heat; simmer, stirring, about 2 minutes or until custard starts to leave side of the pan. Spread mixture into slice pan; cool. Cover; refrigerate 2 hours or until firm.
4 Turn custard onto baking-paper-lined board; using 5cm (2-inch) moon-shaped cutter, cut out 38 shapes. Dust custard shapes with extra flour; shake off excess.
5 Heat oil in large saucepan; deep-fry custard shapes, in batches, until browned lightly. Drain on absorbent paper. Carefully toss hot custard shapes in combined extra sugar and ground cinnamon; serve hot.

prep + cook time 40 minutes (+ standing & refrigeration) **makes** 38
nutritional count per piece 2.5g total fat (0.7g saturated fat); 155kJ (37 cal); 9g carbohydrate; 1.2g protein; 0g fibre
tip Leche frita (or fried milk in English) are deep-fried custard shapes.

Churros

1 cup (250ml) water
1 tablespoon caster (superfine) sugar
90g (3 ounces) butter, chopped coarsely
1 cup (150g) plain (all-purpose) flour
2 eggs
vegetable oil, for deep-frying
aniseed sugar
5 star anise
½ cup (110g) caster (superfine) sugar

1 Make aniseed sugar.
2 Bring the water, sugar and butter to the boil in medium saucepan. Add sifted flour; beat with wooden spoon over high heat until mixture comes away from base and side of pan to form a smooth ball. Transfer mixture to small bowl; beat in eggs, one at a time, with electric mixer until mixture becomes glossy.
3 Spoon mixture into piping bag fitted with a 1cm (½-inch) fluted tube.
4 Heat oil in large saucepan; pipe 6cm (2¼-inch) lengths of batter into oil (cut off lengths with a knife). Deep-fry churros, in batches, about 6 minutes or until browned lightly and crisp. Drain on absorbent paper.
5 Roll churros in aniseed sugar. Serve warm.
aniseed sugar Blend or process ingredients until ground finely.

prep + cook time 30 minutes **makes** 35
nutritional count per churros 3.4g total fat (1.6g saturated fat); 247kJ (59 cal); 6.8g carbohydrate; 0.9g protein; 0.2g fibre

Chocolate churros

60g (2 ounces) unsalted butter
⅔ cup (160ml) water
1⅓ cups (200g) plain (all-purpose) flour
2 tablespoons cocoa powder
1½ tablespoons caster (superfine) sugar
2 eggs
vegetable oil, for deep-frying
½ cup (110g) white (granulated) sugar
2 tablespoons cocoa powder, extra

1 Bring butter and the water to the boil in medium saucepan. Add sifted flour, cocoa and caster sugar; beat with wooden spoon over high heat until mixture comes away from base and side of pan to form a smooth ball. Transfer mixture to small bowl; beat in eggs, one at a time, with electric mixer until mixture becomes glossy.
2 Spoon mixture into piping bag fitted with a 1.5cm (¾-inch) fluted tube.
3 Heat oil in large saucepan; pipe 6cm (2¼-inch) lengths of batter into oil (cut off lengths with a knife). Deep-fry churros, in batches, about 6 minutes or until browned lightly and crisp. Drain on absorbent paper.
4 Roll churros in combined white sugar and sifted extra cocoa.
Serve warm.

prep + cook time 30 minutes **makes** 25
nutritional count per churros 3.9g total fat (1.7g saturated fat); 368kJ (88 cal); 11.7g carbohydrate; 1.6g protein; 0.4g fibre

Melon salad with citrus sugar

½ large pineapple (1kg), peeled, sliced thinly
½ medium rockmelon (850g), peeled, sliced thinly
1.2kg (2½-pound) piece seedless watermelon, peeled, sliced thinly
2 medium oranges (480g), peeled, sliced thinly
citrus sugar
⅓ cup (75g) white (granulated) sugar
1 tablespoon finely grated orange rind
2 teaspoons finely grated lime rind
1 tablespoon finely chopped fresh mint

1 Make citrus sugar.
2 Just before serving, layer fruit on large serving platter, sprinkling citrus sugar between layers.
3 Serve with extra mint leaves, if you like.
citrus sugar Process ingredients until combined.

prep time 20 minutes **serves** 6
nutritional count per serving 0.5g total fat (0g saturated fat);
606kJ (145 cal); 35.2g carbohydrate; 2.4g protein; 4.9g fibre

Chocolate and cinnamon ice-cream

2 cups (500ml) milk
3 cinnamon sticks, halved
185g (6 ounces) dark eating (semi-sweet) chocolate, chopped finely
8 egg yolks
½ cup (110g) caster (superfine) sugar
1¼ cups (310ml) thickened (heavy) cream

1 Stir milk, cinnamon and chocolate, over low heat, in medium saucepan until chocolate is melted. Remove from heat; stand, covered, 5 minutes. Strain into large heatproof jug; discard cinnamon.
2 Beat egg yolks and sugar in small bowl with electric mixer until thick and creamy. With motor operating, gradually add hot chocolate mixture, beating until combined.
3 Return mixture to same cleaned pan; cook, stirring, without boiling, about 15 minutes or until mixture thickens slightly. Transfer mixture to large bowl; cool. Refrigerate about 1 hour or until cold. Stir in cream then pour mixture into loaf pan; cover with foil. Freeze about 3 hours or until firm.
4 Beat ice-cream in large bowl with electric mixer until smooth. Return ice-cream to loaf pan; cover with foil. Freeze about 3 hours or until firm.

prep + cook time 45 minutes (+ standing, refrigeration & freezing)
serves 6
nutritional count per serving 38.8g total fat (22.6g saturated fat); 2002kJ (479 cal); 43.3g carbohydrate; 9.7g protein; 0.4g fibre
tip It is fine to use just one 300ml carton of cream for this recipe.

Citrus rice pudding

2 cups (500ml) no-fat milk
1 vanilla bean, halved lengthways
2 teaspoons finely grated orange rind
1 teaspoon each finely grated lemon rind and lime rind
2 eggs
1 egg white
½ cup (110g) caster (superfine) sugar
1½ cups cooked white medium-grain rice

1 Preheat oven to 160°C/325°F. Grease shallow oval 1.5-litre (6-cup) ovenproof dish.
2 Bring milk, vanilla bean and rinds to the boil in medium saucepan. Remove from heat; stand, covered, 5 minutes. Discard vanilla bean.
3 Meanwhile, whisk eggs, egg white and sugar in medium bowl. Gradually whisk hot milk mixture into egg mixture.
4 Spread rice into dish; pour egg mixture carefully over rice. Place dish in large baking dish; add enough boiling water to baking dish to come halfway up side of pudding dish.
5 Bake pudding about 1 hour or until set.

prep + cook time 1 hour 20 minutes **serves** 8
nutritional count per serving 1.5g total fat (0.5g saturated fat); 573kJ (137 cal); 26.4g carbohydrate; 5.1g protein; 0.2g fibre
tip You need to cook about ½ cup (100g) white medium-grain rice for this recipe.

Spiced oranges with brown sugar toffee

1 cup (220g) firmly packed light brown sugar
1 cup (250ml) water
3 medium oranges (720g), peeled, sliced thickly
3 medium blood oranges (500g), peeled, sliced thickly
¼ teaspoon ground cinnamon
pinch ground cardamom

1 Stir sugar and the water in medium saucepan over low heat until sugar dissolves; bring to the boil. Boil, uncovered, without stirring, about 10 minutes or until mixture is a dark caramel colour. Remove from heat; allow bubbles to subside.
2 Meanwhile, arrange orange slices, overlapping slightly, on large heatproof platter; sprinkle with spices.
3 Pour half the toffee over oranges; pour remaining toffee onto greased oven tray. Stand oranges at room temperature about 2 hours or until toffee dissolves and forms a sauce over oranges. Allow toffee on tray to set at room temperature.
4 Break set toffee into pieces; sprinkle over oranges.

prep + cook time 25 minutes (+ standing) **serves** 6
nutritional count per serving 0.1g total fat (0g saturated fat); 815kJ (195 cal); 46.9g carbohydrate; 1.5g protein; 2.9g fibre
tip When you think the syrup has almost reached the colour we suggest, quickly remove the pan from the heat, remembering that the syrup will continue to cook and darken during this time. Let the bubbles subside, then drop a teaspoon of the syrup into a cup of cold water. The toffee should set the instant it hits the cold water; lift it out and break it with your fingers. If the toffee needs to be harder, then return the mixture to the heat and cook a little more. This test is easy, but a candy thermometer removes all the guess work for you. If you have a candy thermometer, boil the mixture until it reaches 138°C/280°F.

Spiced custards with honey and figs

1 teaspoon whole cloves
1 cinnamon stick
pinch saffron
1¼ cups (310ml) thickened (heavy) cream
⅔ cup (160ml) milk
2 teaspoons gelatine
2 tablespoons caster (superfine) sugar
½ teaspoon vanilla extract
4 medium fresh figs (240g)
2 tablespoons honey

1 Grease four ½-cup (125ml) moulds.
2 Place spices, cream and milk in small saucepan; stand 10 minutes. Sprinkle gelatine and sugar over cream mixture; stir over low heat until gelatine and sugar dissolve. Stir in extract. Strain into medium jug; cool to room temperature. Discard spices.
3 Divide mixture among moulds, cover; refrigerate 3 hours or until set.
4 Quarter figs; stir honey in small saucepan until warm.
5 Turn custards onto serving plates; serve with figs drizzled with honey.

prep + cook time 30 minutes (+ cooling & refrigeration) **serves** 4
nutritional count per serving 29.3g total fat (19.2g saturated fat); 1639kJ (392 cal); 29.1g carbohydrate; 5.1g protein; 1.3g fibre
tip It is fine to use just one 300ml carton of cream for this recipe.

Orange and mango ice

1 large mango (600g), chopped coarsely
2 cups (500ml) orange juice
⅓ cup (75g) caster (superfine) sugar
1 medium orange (240g), cut into thin wedges

1 Blend or process mango until smooth.
2 Stir juice and sugar in medium saucepan over medium heat, without boiling, until sugar dissolves. Stir in mango puree.
3 Pour mixture into loaf pan. Cover with foil; freeze 2 hours. Remove from freezer; using fork, scrape the frozen mixture from sides and base of pan. Cover; freeze a further 6 hours or until firm.
4 Stand granita at room temperature 10 minutes. Using fork, scrape the surface and spoon into chilled serving bowls. Serve granita with orange wedges.

prep + cook time 20 minutes (+ freezing) **serves** 4
nutritional count per serving 0.4g total fat (0g saturated fat); 840kJ (201 cal); 45.2g carbohydrate; 2.2g protein; 2.7g fibre

Chocolate and orange polenta cake

1 cup (220g) caster (superfine)
  sugar
1 ½ cups (375ml) water
2 small oranges (240g), sliced
¼ cup (60ml) water, extra
125g (4 ounces) butter, softened
1 tablespoon finely grated
  orange rind
1 cup (220g) firmly packed
  light brown sugar
3 eggs
½ cup (35g) plain (all-purpose)
  flour

½ cup (75g) self-raising flour
½ teaspoon bicarbonate of soda
  (baking soda)
½ cup (50g) cocoa powder
½ cup (60g) ground almonds
½ cup (125g) polenta
⅓ cup (80g) sour cream
¼ cup (60ml) orange juice
90g (3 ounces) dark eating
  (semi-sweet) chocolate,
  chopped finely

1 Preheat oven to 180°C/ 350°F. Grease deep 20cm (8-inch) round cake pan; line base and side with two layers of baking paper.
2 Stir caster sugar and the water in large frying pan over medium heat, without boiling, until sugar dissolves. Bring to the boil. Reduce heat; simmer, uncovered, without stirring, 5 minutes or until syrup thickens slightly. Add orange slices; simmer gently, uncovered, about 7 minutes or until rind is tender, turning slices halfway through cooking time.
3 Remove from heat; using tongs, lift orange slices from syrup and place in base of pan, slightly overlapping each slice. Reserve syrup.
4 Add the extra water to reserved syrup in pan; bring to the boil. Reduce heat; simmer, uncovered, without stirring, until syrup is a light honey colour. Pour two-thirds of hot syrup over orange slices; reserve remaining syrup.
5 Beat butter, rind and brown sugar in small bowl with electric mixer until light and fluffy. Beat in eggs, one at a time. Transfer to large bowl; stir in sifted flours, soda and cocoa, then ground almonds, polenta, sour cream, juice and chocolate. Carefully spread mixture over oranges in pan.
6 Bake cake about 1 ¼ hours. Stand cake in pan 15 minutes; turn onto serving plate. Spoon reserved syrup over oranges.

prep + cook time 2 hours **serves** 8
nutritional count per serving 27.5g total fat (14.4g saturated fat); 2429kJ (581 cal); 87.1g carbohydrate; 9.2g protein; 2.7g fibre
serving suggestion Ice-cream or cream.

Little orange flans

1¼ cups (275g) caster (superfine) sugar
½ cup (125ml) water
¼ cup (60ml) orange juice
2 cups (500ml) low-fat milk
3 eggs
3 egg yolks
1 teaspoon vanilla extract
2 teaspoons finely grated orange rind

1 Preheat oven to 160°C/325°F.
2 Combine ¾ cup of the sugar with the water in medium saucepan;
stir over low heat, without boiling, until sugar dissolves. Bring to the boil;
boil, uncovered, without stirring, until mixture is caramel in colour. Remove
from heat; add juice (some of the toffee will set; stir over low heat until
toffee melts). Divide mixture among six ½-cup (125ml) ovenproof dishes.
3 Bring milk to the boil in small saucepan. Whisk remaining sugar, eggs,
egg yolks and extract in medium bowl; gradually whisk hot milk into
egg mixture. Stir in rind; pour mixture over toffee in dishes.
4 Place dishes in medium baking dish; add enough boiling water to
come halfway up the sides of flan dishes. Bake about 45 minutes or
until custards set. Remove flan dishes from baking dish; cool 10 minutes.
Cover; refrigerate overnight.
5 Using fingers, gently ease each custard away from side of dish then
invert onto individual serving plates.

prep + cook time 1 hour 20 minutes (+ refrigeration) **makes** 6
nutritional count per flan 3.8g total fat (1.8g saturated);
1170kJ (280 cal); 52.8g carbohydrate; 7.9g protein; 0.1g fibre

Citrus salad with lime and mint ice

2 medium oranges (480g)
2 small pink grapefruits (700g)
⅓ cup finely chopped fresh mint
2 tablespoons icing (confectioners') sugar
1 tablespoon lime juice
2 cups ice cubes

1 Segment oranges and grapefruit into medium bowl.
2 Blend or process mint, sugar, juice and ice until ice is crushed.
3 Serve fruit with ice.

prep time 15 minutes **serves** 4
nutritional count per serving 0.4g total fat (0g saturated fat);
385kJ (92 cal); 18.1g carbohydrate; 2.1g protein; 2.7g fibre

glossary

almonds see page 10

blanched brown skins removed.

ground also called almond meal.

slivered small pieces cut lengthways.

artichokes

globe large flower-bud of a member of the thistle family; it has tough petal-like leaves, and is edible in part when cooked.

hearts tender centre of the globe artichoke; is obtained after the choke is removed. Cooked hearts are available in brine or marinated in oil.

jerusalem neither from Jerusalem nor an artichoke, this crunchy brown-skinned tuber tastes a bit like a water chestnut and belongs to the sunflower family. Eat raw in salads or cooked like potatoes.

bay leaves aromatic leaves from the bay tree available fresh or dried; adds a strong, slightly peppery flavour.

beans

broad (fava) also called windsor and horse beans; available dried, fresh, canned and frozen. Fresh should be peeled twice (discard outer green pod and beige-green inner shell); the frozen beans have had their pods removed but the beige shell still needs removal.

cannellini small white bean similar to other *phaseolus vulgaris* varieties (great northern, navy or haricot). Available dried or canned.

green also called french or string beans (although the tough string they once had has generally been bred out of them), this long thin fresh bean is consumed in its entirety once cooked.

kidney medium-size red bean, slightly floury in texture yet sweet in flavour; sold dried or canned, it's found in bean mixes and is used in chilli con carne.

white a generic term we use for canned or dried cannellini, haricot, navy or great northern beans.

beef, skirt lean, flavourful coarse-grained cut from the inner thigh. Needs slow-cooking; good for stews or casseroles.

beetroot (beets) firm, round root vegetable.

bicarbonate of soda also called baking soda.

blood orange a virtually seedless citrus fruit with blood-red-streaked rind and flesh; sweet, non-acidic, salmon-coloured pulp and juice with slight strawberry or raspberry overtones. The rind is not as bitter as an ordinary orange.

breadcrumbs

packaged prepared fine-textured but crunchy white breadcrumbs; good for coating foods that are to be fried.

stale crumbs made by grating, blending or processing 1- or 2-day-old bread.

butter we use salted butter unless stated.

caperberries olive-sized fruit formed after the buds of the caper bush have flowered; they are usually sold pickled in a vinegar brine with stalks intact.

capers grey-green buds of a warm climate shrub, sold dried and salted or pickled in a vinegar brine; tiny young ones (baby capers) are available in brine or dried in salt.

capsicum (bell pepper) see page 10

cardamom a spice native to India and used extensively in its cuisine; can be purchased in pod, seed or ground form. Has a distinctive aromatic, sweetly rich flavour and is one of the world's most expensive spices.

cayenne pepper a thin-fleshed, long, very hot dried red chilli, usually available ground.

cheese

bocconcini from the diminutive of "boccone", meaning mouthful in

Italian; walnut-sized, baby mozzarella, a delicate, semi-soft, white cheese. Sold fresh, it spoils rapidly; refrigerate in brine for 1 or 2 days.

fetta Greek in origin; a crumbly textured goat's- or sheep's-milk cheese with a sharp, salty taste.

goat's made from goat's milk; has an earthy, strong taste. Available soft, crumbly and firm, in various shapes and sizes, and sometimes rolled in ash or herbs.

manchego see page 10

mozzarella soft, spun-curd cheese; traditionally made from water-buffalo milk. Now generally made from cow's milk, it is the most popular pizza cheese because of its low melting point and elasticity when heated.

parmesan also called parmigiano; a hard, grainy cow's-milk cheese originating in the Parma region of Italy. The curd is salted in brine for a month then aged for up to 2 years.

ricotta soft, sweet, moist, white cow's-milk cheese with a low fat content (8.5 per cent) and a slightly grainy texture. Its name roughly translates as "cooked again" and refers to ricotta's manufacture from a whey that is itself a by-product of other cheese making.

chervil also called cicily; mildly fennel-flavoured member of the parsley family with curly dark-green leaves. Available both fresh and dried but, like all herbs, is best used fresh; it loses its delicate flavour the longer it's cooked.

chicken

breast fillet breast halved, skinned, boned.

drumettes small fleshy part of the wing between shoulder and elbow, trimmed to resemble a drumstick.

drumsticks leg with skin and bone intact.

small chicken also called spatchcock or poussin; no more than 6 weeks old, weighing a maximum of 500g. Spatchcock is also a cooking term to describe splitting poultry open, flattening and grilling.

tenderloins thin strip of meat lying just under the breast.

thigh cutlets thigh with skin and centre bone intact; sometimes found skinned with bone intact.

thigh fillets thigh with skin and centre bone removed.

chickpeas (garbanzo beans) an irregularly round, sandy-coloured legume. Available canned or dried (soak several hours in water before use). See also page 11

chilli use rubber gloves when handling fresh chillies as they can burn your skin. We use unseeded chillies as the seeds contain the heat.

ancho mild, dried chillies commonly used in Mexican cooking.

chipotle pronounced cheh-pote-lay. The name used for jalapeño chillies once they've been dried and smoked. Having a deep, intensely smokey flavour, rather than a searing heat, chipotles are dark brown, almost black in colour and wrinkled in appearance.

flakes also sold as crushed chilli; dehydrated deep-red extremely fine slices and whole seeds.

green any unripened chilli; also particular varieties that are ripe when green, such as jalapeño, habanero, poblano or serrano.

jalapeño pronounced hah-lah-pain-yo. Fairly hot, medium-sized, plump, dark green chilli; available pickled, sold canned or bottled, and fresh, from greengrocers.

chocolate, dark eating (semi-sweet) contains a high percentage of cocoa liquor and cocoa butter, and little added sugar. It is ideal for use in desserts and cakes.

chorizo see page 8

cinnamon available in pieces (sticks or quills) and ground into powder. See also page 11

cloves dried flower buds of a tropical tree; used whole or ground. They have a strong scent and taste so use sparingly.

cocoa powder also known as unsweetened cocoa.

cornflour also called cornstarch. Made from corn or wheat.

cream

pouring also known as pure cream. It has no additives, and contains a minimum fat content of 35 per cent.

thickened a whipping cream that contains a thickener (minimum fat content of 35 per cent).

cucumber, lebanese also known as european or burpless cucumber; short, slender and thin-skinned.

cumin also called zeera or comino; resembling caraway in size, cumin is the dried seed of a parsley-related plant with a spicy, almost curry-like flavour. Available dried as seeds or ground.

dill also called dill weed; used fresh or dried, in seed form or ground. Its feathery, frond-like fresh leaves are grassier and more subtle than the dried version or the seeds.

eggplant also called aubergine. Ranging in size from tiny to very large and in colour from pale green to deep purple. Can also be purchased char-grilled, packed in oil, in jars.

eggs we use large (60g) chicken eggs. If a recipe calls for raw or barely cooked eggs, exercise caution if there is a salmonella problem in your area, particularly in food eaten by children and pregnant women.

endive, curly also called frisee, a curly-leafed green vegetable, mainly used in salads.

fennel also called finocchio or anise; a crunchy green vegetable slightly resembling celery. Dried fennel seeds are also available; they have a stronger licorice flavour.

figs are best eaten in peak season, at the height of summer. Vary in skin and flesh colour according to type not ripeness. When ripe, figs should be unblemished and bursting with flesh.

flour

plain unbleached wheat flour is the best for baking: the gluten content ensures a strong dough, which produces a light result.

rice very fine, almost powdery, gluten-free flour; made from ground white rice.

self-raising plain or wholemeal flour with baking powder and salt added; make at home in the proportion of 1 cup flour to 2 teaspoons baking powder.

gelatine we use dried (powdered) gelatine; it's also available in sheet form called leaf gelatine. Three teaspoons of dried gelatine (8g or one sachet) is about the same as four sheets.

honey honey sold in a squeezable container is not suitable for the recipes in this book.

jamón see page 9

kumara the Polynesian name of an orange-fleshed sweet potato often confused with yam; good baked, boiled, mashed or fried similarly to other potatoes.

lentils (red, brown, yellow) dried pulses often identified by and named after their colour. Eaten by cultures all over the world, most famously perhaps in the dhals of India, lentils have high food value.

mayonnaise we use whole-egg mayonnaise; a commercial product of high quality made with whole eggs and labelled as such.

milk we use full-cream homogenised milk unless stated otherwise.

mizuna Japanese in origin; these frizzy green salad leaves have a delicate mustard flavour.

mushrooms

button small, cultivated white mushrooms with a mild flavour. When a recipe in this book calls for an unspecified mushroom, use button.

flat large and flat with a rich earthy flavour. Sometimes misnamed field mushrooms which are wild mushrooms.

swiss brown also called roman or cremini. Light to dark brown mushrooms with full-bodied flavour.

mustard

dijon also called french. Pale brown, creamy, distinctively flavoured, fairly mild french mustard.

wholegrain also called seeded. A French-style coarse-grain mustard made from crushed mustard seeds and dijon-style french mustard.

nutmeg a strong and pungent spice ground from the dried nut of a native Indonesian tree. Usually found ground, the flavour is more intense from a whole nut, available from spice shops, so it's best to grate your own. Found in mixed spice mixtures.

oil

cooking spray we use a cholesterol-free spray made from canola oil.

olive made from ripened olives. Extra virgin and virgin are the first and second press, respectively, and are therefore considered the best; the "extra light" or "light" on other types refers to taste not fat levels. See also page 8

vegetable any number of oils from plant rather than animal fats.

olives see page 9

onion

green also called scallion or (incorrectly) shallot; an immature onion picked before the bulb has formed, having a long, bright-green edible stalk.

red also called spanish, red spanish or bermuda onion; a sweet-flavoured, large, purple-red onion.

shallots also called french shallots, golden shallots or eschalots. Small and elongated, with a brown-skin, they grow in tight clusters similar to garlic.

oranges see page 11

oregano also called wild marjoram; has a woody stalk and clumps of tiny, dark-green leaves. Has a pungent, peppery flavour.

paprika ground dried, sweet red capsicum (bell pepper); varieties available include sweet, hot, mild and smoked.

pine nuts also known as pignoli; not a nut but a small, cream-coloured kernel from pine cones. They are best roasted before use to bring out the flavour.

polenta also known as cornmeal; a flour-like cereal made of dried corn (maize). Also the dish made from it.

pomegranate dark-red, leathery-skinned fresh fruit about the size of an orange filled with hundreds of seeds, each wrapped in an edible lucent-crimson pulp having a unique tangy sweet-sour flavour.

potato

baby new also called chats; not a separate variety but an early harvest with very thin skin. Good unpeeled steamed, eaten hot or cold in salads.

bintje oval, creamy skin, yellow flesh; good all-purpose potato, great baked and fried, good in salads.

kipfler small, finger-shaped, nutty flavour; great baked and in salads.

russet burbank long and oval, rough white skin with shallow eyes, white flesh; good for baking and frying.

389

preserved lemon rind lemons preserved in salt and lemon juice or water. Sold in jars at delis and some supermarkets; once opened, keep refrigerated. To use, remove and discard pulp, squeeze juice from rind; slice rind thinly. Use the rind only and rinse well under cold water before using.

quail related to the pheasant and partridge; a small, delicate-flavoured farmed game bird ranging in weight from 250g to 300g.

radicchio Italian in origin; a member of the chicory family. The dark burgundy leaves and strong, bitter flavour can be cooked or eaten raw in salads.

rice

arborio small, round grain rice well-suited to absorb a large amount of liquid; the high level of starch makes it suitable for risottos, giving the dish its classic creaminess.

bomba short-grain Spanish rice used in paella recipes; absorbs about three times its volume in liquid. See also page 8

calasparra see page 8

long-grain elongated grains that remain separate when cooked; this is the most popular steaming rice in Asia.

short-grain fat, almost round grain with a high starch content; tends to clump together when cooked.

white is hulled and polished rice, can be short-or long-grained.

roasting/toasting nuts and dried coconut can be roasted in the oven to restore their fresh flavour and release aromatic oils; spread evenly onto an oven tray, roast in a moderate oven about 5 minutes. Desiccated coconut, pine nuts and sesame seeds roast more evenly if stirred over low heat in a heavy-based frying pan; their natural oils help turn them golden.

rocket (arugula) also called rucola; peppery green leaf eaten raw or used in cooking. Baby rocket leaves are smaller and less peppery.

saffron see page 9

seafood

anchovies see page 9

marinara mix a mixture of uncooked, chopped seafood available from fishmarkets and fishmongers.

mussels should only be bought from a reliable fish market: they must be tightly closed when bought, indicating they are alive. Before cooking, scrub shells with a strong brush to remove beards;

do not eat any that do not open after cooking.

octopus usually tenderised before you buy them; both octopus and squid require either long slow cooking (for large molluscs) or quick cooking over high heat (for small molluscs) – anything in between will make the octopus tough and rubbery.

prawns (shrimp) can be bought uncooked (green) or cooked, with or without shells.

sardines see page 9

scallops a type of bivalve; often eaten raw or barely seared, they should never be cooked more than 30 seconds as they will lose their juicy tenderness and be tough.

squid also known as calamari; a type of mollusc. Buy squid hoods to make preparation and cooking faster.

swordfish also called broadbill. Substitute with yellowfin or bluefin tuna or mahi mahi.

white fish non-oily fish; includes bream, flathead, whiting, snapper, redfish, dhufish and ling.

semolina coarsely ground flour milled from durum wheat.

sherry see page 10

silver beet also called swiss chard and incorrectly, spinach;

has fleshy stalks and large leaves.

spinach also called english spinach and incorrectly, silver beet. Baby spinach leaves are best eaten raw in salads; the larger leaves should be added last to soups, stews and stir-fries, and should be cooked until barely wilted.

star anise a dried star-shaped pod whose seeds have an astringent aniseed flavour; used to flavour stocks and marinades.

sugar

brown a soft, finely granulated sugar retaining molasses for colour and flavour.

caster also called superfine or finely granulated table sugar.

icing also known as confectioners' sugar or powdered sugar; pulverised granulated sugar crushed together with a small amount of cornflour.

pure icing also known as confectioners' sugar or powdered sugar.

tomato

bottled pasta sauce a prepared sauce; often a blend of tomatoes, herbs and spices.

canned whole peeled tomatoes in natural juices; available crushed, chopped or diced. Use undrained.

cherry also called tiny tim or tom thumb; small and round.

egg (plum) also called roma; smallish, oval-shaped tomatoes.

paste triple-concentrated tomato puree used to flavour soups, stews, sauces and casseroles.

puree canned pureed tomatoes (not tomato paste); substitute with fresh peeled and pureed tomatoes.

semi-dried partially dried tomato pieces in olive oil; softer and juicier than sun-dried, these are not preserved so do not keep as long as sun-dried.

sun-dried tomato pieces dried with salt; this dehydrates the tomato, concentrating the flavour. We use sun-dried tomatoes in oil, unless stated otherwise.

turmeric also called kamin; is a rhizome related to galangal and ginger. Must be grated or pounded to release its acrid aroma and pungent flavour. Known for the golden colour it imparts, fresh turmeric can be substituted with the more commonly found dried powder.

vanilla

bean dried, long, thin pod; the minuscule black

seeds inside are used to impart a vanilla flavour.

extract obtained from vanilla beans infused in water; a non-alcoholic version of essence.

vinegar

balsamic originally from Modena, Italy, there are now many on the market ranging in pungency and quality. Quality can be determined up to a point by price; use the most expensive sparingly.

cider made from fermented apples.

sherry see page 10

wine made from red or white wine.

watercress one of the cress family, a large group of peppery greens used raw in salads, dips and sandwiches, or cooked in soups. Highly perishable, so it must be used as soon as possible after purchase.

witlof also called belgian endive; related to and confused with chicory. A versatile vegetable, it tastes good cooked and raw.

yeast (dried and fresh), a raising agent. Granular (7g sachets) and fresh (20g blocks) yeast can almost always be used interchangeably.

zucchini also called courgette; harvested when young, its edible flowers can be stuffed and deep-fried.

index

393

conversion chart

MEASURES

One Australian metric measuring cup holds approximately 250ml, one Australian metric tablespoon holds 20ml, one Australian metric teaspoon holds 5ml.

The difference between one country's measuring cups and another's is within a two- or three-teaspoon variance, and will not affect your cooking results.North America, New Zealand and the United Kingdom use a 15ml tablespoon.

All cup and spoon measurements are level. The most accurate way of measuring dry ingredients is to weigh them. When measuring liquids, use a clear glass or plastic jug with the metric markings.

We use large eggs with an average weight of 60g.

LIQUID MEASURES

METRIC	IMPERIAL
30ml	1 fluid oz
60ml	2 fluid oz
100ml	3 fluid oz
125ml	4 fluid oz
150ml	5 fluid oz (¼ pint/1 gill)
190ml	6 fluid oz
250ml	8 fluid oz
300ml	10 fluid oz (½ pint)
500ml	16 fluid oz
600ml	20 fluid oz (1 pint)
1000ml (1 litre)	1¾ pints

LENGTH MEASURES

METRIC	IMPERIAL
3mm	⅛in
6mm	¼in
1cm	½in
2cm	¾in
2.5cm	1in
5cm	2in
6cm	2½in
8cm	3in
10cm	4in
13cm	5in
15cm	6in
18cm	7in
20cm	8in
23cm	9in
25cm	10in
28cm	11in
30cm	12in (1ft)

DRY MEASURES

METRIC	IMPERIAL
15g	½oz
30g	1oz
60g	2oz
90g	3oz
125g	4oz (¼lb)
155g	5oz
185g	6oz
220g	7oz
250g	8oz (½lb)
280g	9oz
315g	10oz
345g	11oz
375g	12oz (¾lb)
410g	13oz
440g	14oz
470g	15oz
500g	16oz (1lb)
750g	24oz (1½lb)
1kg	32oz (2lb)

OVEN TEMPERATURES

The oven temperatures in this book are for conventional ovens;
if you have a fan-forced oven, decrease the temperature by 10-20 degrees.

	°C (CELSIUS)	°F (FAHRENHEIT)
Very slow	120	250
Slow	150	300
Moderately slow	160	325
Moderate	180	350
Moderately hot	200	400
Hot	220	425
Very hot	240	475

First published in 2011 by ACP Magazines Ltd,

a division of Nine Entertainment Co.

54 Park St, Sydney

GPO Box 4088, Sydney, NSW 2001.

phone (02) 9282 8618; fax (02) 9267 9438

acpbooks@acpmagazines.com.au; www.acpbooks.com.au

ACP BOOKS

General Manager - Christine Whiston

Associate Publisher - Seymour Cohen

Editor-in-Chief - Susan Tomnay

Creative Director - Hieu Chi Nguyen

Food Director - Pamela Clark

Published and Distributed in the United Kingdom by Octopus Publishing Group

Endeavour House

189 Shaftesbury Avenue

London WC2H 8JY

United Kingdom

phone (+44)(0)207 632 5400; fax (+44)(0)207 632 5405

info@octopus-publishing.co.uk;

www.octopusbooks.co.uk

Printed by Toppan Printing Co., China

International foreign language rights, Brian Cearnes, ACP Books bcearnes@acpmagazines.com.au

A catalogue record for this book is available from the British Library.

ISBN 978-1-74245-109-1